BRITISH GASTRONOMY

The Rise of Great Restaurants

BRITISH GASTRONOMY

The Rise of Great Restaurants

GREGORY HOUSTON BOWDEN

1975
CHATTO & WINDUS
LONDON

Published by
Chatto and Windus Ltd
42 William IV Street
London W.C.2N 4DF

*

Clarke, Irwin & Co Ltd
Toronto

ISBN   0 7011 2082 7

Printed in Great Britain by
Fletcher & Son Ltd, Norwich

For my parents, my brothers
and Richard McLaren, all of
whom share my enthusiasm
for the subject of this book

CONTENTS

COLOUR PLATES

ILLUSTRATIONS

FOREWORD

I wrote this book for pleasure and it is, frankly, not intended to be a text-book. That is to say, you will not in most cases find a complete history of every restaurant mentioned in the text from the day it opened until the present time; instead, restaurants are mentioned at whatever time they were most significant in the story of the development of gastronomy in Britain.

I am worried that some people may feel aggrieved that I have left out their favourite restaurant. The answer to this is that I have had to leave out a number of my own favourite places because they did not seem significant in the story. But then, this is not a guide and so the fact that a restaurant is missed out does not in any way suggest that it is not an extremely good place!

I am also concerned that some readers will wonder why I have not told the story of the rise of good restaurants in Wales and Northern Ireland in a book which has the word 'British' in the title. In answer to this, I must explain that although there are a number of good restaurants in both these parts of the United Kingdom, gastronomy is not sufficiently established as yet for there to be a real story to tell and I do not wish to act merely as a guide.

I could not have written this book without the help of the following (many of whom were kind enough to provide photographs), and I would like to express to them my sincere thanks:

Mr. Claude Morny and Mr. Harry Yoxall (International Wine and Food Society); Miss Tin Forbes and the staff of the London Library; Mr. Michael Ross (Cottage-in-the-Woods Hotel, Malvern); Mr. Massara (Quaglinos); Mr. Negri (The Empress); Mr. Osborne (Hyde Park Hotel); Mr. Morton Neal, Mr. Dunas and Mr. Simmons (Connaught Hotel); Miss Susie Orde (Savoy Hotel); Mr. Malcolm Reid and Mr. Colin Long (The Box Tree Cottage, Ilkley); Mr. Tom Benson and Mr. Beecher Moore (Parkes' Restaurant); Mrs. Grete Hobbs (Inverlochy Castle, Fort William); Mr. and Mrs. Keith Knight (Houstoun House, Uphall); Mr. and Mrs. Patrick Stevenson (The Horn of Plenty, Gulworthy); Miss Blatter,

Mr. Willy Smith and Mr. Barnett (Boulestin); Mr. George Perry-Smith and Miss Joyce Molyneux (The Hole in the Wall, Bath); Mr. Albert Roux (Le Poulbot and Le Gavroche); Mr. and Mrs. Paul Leyton (The Miners' Arms, Priddy); Mr. Shura Shihwarg (The Golden Duck, London); Mr. T. H. Young (Rendezvous Restaurants); Mr. Moulin (British Transport Hotels); Mr. David Levin (Capital Hotel, London;) M. Bonvin (Kettner's Restaurant); Mr. Deamer (Hind's Head, Bray).

Also the following:

Lord Cecil Douglas; Mr. Egon Ronay; Mr. Quentin Crewe; Mr. Nicholas Clarke; Miss Molly Lowrance; Mr. Walter Baxter; Mr. Bill Stoughton; Dr. Hilary James; Mme Prunier; Mr. Kenneth Lo; Mr. Robert Carrier; Mr. Norman Pigache; Mr. Strone Macpherson.

I would also like to thank Miss Georgina Fuller (photographic research), Mr. N. S. Lilley (Queensway Studios, Thame), Mr. Sully and Mr. Watts (Barley Ltd., Thame) for photographic processing, and lastly my father, Sir Frank Bowden, for his advice and encouragement.

Finally, I would like to thank Roberto of Lockets Restaurant for feeding me so well while this book was being written, and I offer this wish to all who read my book – *Bon Appétit!*

G.A.H.B.

Chapter 1

INTRODUCTION

ALTHOUGH it has been fashionable until recently to think of Britain as something approaching a gastronomic wilderness, there can be little doubt that the title no longer fits and while not everyone would be so outspoken as Egon Ronay, who declared in his 1971 *Guide* that 'London has clearly established itself as the world's gastronomic centre', many people would agree that the best restaurants in Britain are among the very best in the world outside France. In view of the many foreign influences we have encountered over the years it was perhaps inevitable that we should be a gastronomic country and we also produce some of the finest raw materials for the kitchen, especially meat, fish and game. It is also fashionable to say that we are a nation with no cuisine of our own, but that is not true either: puddings and pies both sweet and savoury, tripe and onions, Yorkshire pudding and roast grouse, for instance, are all truly British fare. In the realm of soups we have cock-a-leekie, pea soup, Scotch broth and mulligatawny and in fish dishes, fried whitebait, smoked salmon and potted shrimps. Nor can anyone deny that we created the English breakfast. Even when we turn to sauces, which are generally accepted as being almost exclusively a French preserve, we find many examples of our own inventions such as mint, caper, horseradish and Cumberland sauce. No, the British should not be ashamed of their national cuisine which at its best is splendid, but that is beside the point. For true artistry we have to turn to France since no plate of whitebait can really be compared with the exquisite delicacy of *quenelles de brochet* nor our treacle tart with a fresh raspberry *soufflé*. Now that a number of British chefs are capable of cooking French dishes extremely well and of offering them on their menus together with expertly cooked examples of our own dishes, our best restaurants are, as I have said, among the best in the world outside France. But England, in spite of this, is not a gastronomic country in the sense that France is. Our factory workers and farm labourers do not rush off at midday to eat *pâté*, steak with *béarnaise* and *crème caramel* like many of their French counterparts. The reason for this is not so much a lack of money as a lack of tradition and the fundamental cause seems to lie in the growth of Puritanism in the late 16th century. As far as good eating is concerned Britain has never fully recovered from the Puritans' condemnation of the pleasures of the flesh. However, if we are to understand fully how Britain has come to have a number of out-standing restaurants, we must look back way beyond the Puritan era and see what first developed the culinary art in our woad-painted ancestors.

It seems that the first people to treat cookery as an art were the Ancient Greeks and many of their ideas travelled to Rome in the days when the Empire was becoming rich and idle and there they were incorporated into the local cuisine. Indeed, the Romans began to be immensely interested in their food so that although our native population must have found it extremely disagreeable to be invaded by them, they were at least privileged to be invaded by a gastronomic nation. The vastness of the Roman Empire enabled those who lived at its heart in Rome to have access to a hitherto unheard-of variety of ingredients which were brought to the capital from distant territories. This, together with a plentiful supply of slave labour to prepare the ingredients and transform them into culinary masterpieces under the watchful eye of a highly paid master-chef, enabled rich Romans to eat very well.

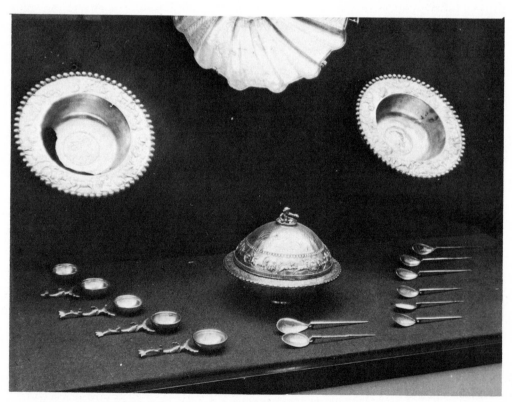

1. Part of the Mildenhall treasure – a set of Roman silver plate found at Mildenhall, Suffolk, buried together with coins dating from A.D. 407–11.

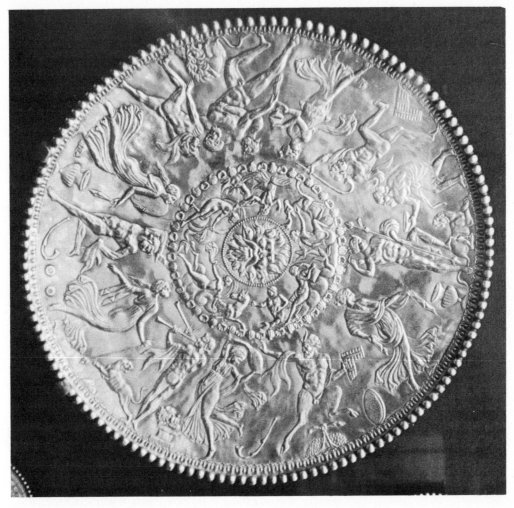

2. A large dish from the Mildenhall treasure.

Fortunately, enough Roman literary works have survived to give us quite a good idea of what the cuisine was like and it is perhaps surprising to find that many of the dishes they ate sound delicious even to modern ears although their habit of using *liquamen*, a sauce made of putrefied fish intestines, with almost everything they ate, seems less attractive. Our best source of information about Roman cookery is a complete cookery book written by M. Gabius Apicius. Seneca tells us that one day Apicius decided to count up his fortune and found that he had spent one hundred million sesterces on food over a period of years and was now down to his last ten million. Being a true and devoted gourmet he immediately decided to take his own life rather than risk having to eat less well. The book contains hundreds of recipes and several ways are suggested for preparing every kind of flesh, fowl, and fish as well as vegetables. Puddings are also afforded plenty of space. I cannot possibly go into great detail but equally I cannot resist giving a few examples of his recipes:

Fricassee of Pork with Apricots: Put in the saucepan oil, *liquamen*, wine, chop in dry shallot, add diced shoulder of pork cooked previously. When all this is cooked pound pepper, dried mint, cummin and dill, moisten with honey, *liquamen*, a little vinegar and some cooking liquor. Mix well. Bring to the boil and let it boil until done. Crumble in pastry to bind. Sprinkle with pepper to serve.

Sauce for roast Crane of Duck: Pound pepper, lovage, origan, *liquamen*, honey, a little vinegar and a little cooking oil. Cook well. Add cornflour (to bind) and put into the sauce slices of boiled cucumber. Boil. If available, add cooked pigs trotters and chicken livers.

Note on cooking birds: You give a bird a greater flavour and make it more nourishing if you wrap it in pastry made from oil and flour and cook it in the oven.

Puddings: Take best wheat flour and cook it in hot water so that it forms a very hard paste, then spread it on a plate. When cold, cut it up for sweets and fry in best oil. Lift out, pour honey over and sprinkle with pepper then serve.

Another Pudding: Remove the crust from a wheaten loaf, break up into fairly large morsels, steep in milk, fry in oil, pour honey over and serve.

Other recipes found in Apicius' masterpiece include lobster rissoles, dishes with truffles, roast sucking-pig stuffed with pastry and honey and all kinds of sausages. But Apicius is by no means the only Roman who wrote about food although he is the only one who actually described how to prepare it. Petronius speaks of dormice garnished with honey and poppy-seeds; Macrobius of a compôte of river-birds and Martial says, 'The pale bean will accompany the red streaked bacon'.

To understand fully just how fond of their food the Romans were we need only remember that Cato the Censor found it necessary to reproach his fellow-countrymen for paying more for a single red mullet than for a cow. Inevitably some of the interest in food began to filter through to the Ancient Britons in the centuries that followed the Roman conquest, though they, as the underdogs, would not have eaten as well as their Roman masters.

After about 400 years of occupation, the Romans found matters becoming difficult at home and accordingly withdrew all their forces from Britain.

This gave the Anglo-Saxons the opportunity to invade us and bring with them a new set of ideas about cooking. The most obvious change under the Anglo-Saxons was that fewer spices and more pot herbs were used, though the rich undoubtedly had access to some spices such as cinnamon and ginger. Otherwise herbs such as hyssop, fennel, rosemary, parsley and coriander were widely grown and onions were popular too. Although they were less civilized than the Romans, the Anglo-Saxons were not devoid of good taste and they too valued good cooks very highly and, like their Roman predecessors, paid them well. Favourite dishes included stews flavoured with pot herbs, pigeon cooked in a piquant vinegar sauce, peas sweetened with honey and fatty broth to keep the cold out. Naturally, they enjoyed all types of game and fish and they kept pigs. Beef was probably not very often eaten as cows were kept for their milk, and oxen to pull ploughs. Nor was mutton regularly eaten, for sheep were kept almost exclusively for their wool.

1066, that date we all seem able to remember, brought the third major invasion of England and hence the third important foreign influence on our cooking.

The Norman cuisine was in fact very similar to the Roman one and so the change was not very dramatic. Perhaps a little more spice and fewer herbs began to be used and we know of such mouth-watering dishes as pork broiled on red embers with garlic and spit-roasted goose with verjuice and garlic sauce. We also hear of such delicacies as fish simmered in white wine and herbs so that we must conclude that Norman cooking was, even by today's standards, very acceptable. We were never invaded again after 1066 but foreign influences nevertheless continued to make themselves felt in less violent ways, as we can see by looking at the first great English cookery book, *The Forme of Cury*. This book was drawn up by chefs of Richard II who, judging from this work, must have a good claim to be called our first gourmet king. Indeed, it was not for nothing that he was known throughout the civilized world as 'The best and Royalist vyander of all Christian Kings'. He employed 2,000 cooks, with a further 200 helpers.

The exact date of *The Forme of Cury* is not known though it seems very likely that the 196 recipes it contains were collected throughout Richard's reign which lasted from 1377 to 1399. The recipes are remarkably exotic and call for the widespread use of spices such as pepper, cinnamon, ginger and nutmeg. Foreign influence may be seen in such examples as the recipe for oysters cooked in Greek wine and the recipe for *zabaglione*. There is no mention made of plain roast meats at Richard's table, everything being more made-up than that, and a typical main course was *mawmenee* which was minced pheasant prepared with Greek wine, cinnamon, cloves, ginger and sugar. However, roasts were almost certainly widely eaten outside the court and by this time both beef and mutton would have featured on the list of roast meats in regular use. Probably the most serious gap in the diet at this time was the lack of vegetables which had become increasingly less popular after the Norman invasion and were destined to remain so until the 16th century. Fruits were not very much eaten either.

Richard's successor, Henry IV, was almost equally gourmet-minded, as is shown by some of the succulent dishes served at his wedding-feast. They included *Braun en Peuerade*, slices of meat cooked in a sweet and sour sauce, *Viaund Ryal*, a *purée* of rice and mulberries sweetened with honey and flavoured with wine and spices, and a delicious sweet called *Crustarde Lumbarde* which was a sort of pie made from cream, eggs, dates, prunes and sugar.

The Tudor period is an interesting one in the story of the development of the culinary art in England for it was then that fruits and vegetables came into more regular use. There were, of course, those who still felt that the only real food for a man was meat and that vegetables should be left for the peasants, but others accepted the teaching of the great Andrew Borde, a Catholic monk who wrote about diet. It was he who said: 'It is a commodious and pleasant thing to a mansion to have an orchard of sundry fruits, but it is more commodious to have a fair garden, replete with herbs of aromatic and redolent savour.' By herbs he meant vegetables in general. We know from contemporary writers such as Gerarde that no less than thirty salad herbs were in general use in Elizabethan times and that is far more than we use today. In addition to all the usual vegetables such as spinach and beets, the Elizabethans used dandelion leaves, leaves of musk-roses, orach, endives and tarragon. However, because of the Puritan influence which made talking and thinking about food seem sinful, English gastronomy did not develop at all during Elizabeth's reign and this was a tragedy since it was just at this time that French cooking began to move ahead by leaps and bounds. This was because, in the 16th century by far the best cooking in the world was to be found in Italy and it was therefore a great day for French gastronomy when, in 1533, Catherine de Medici married Henry II of France and took with her to France some of the finest cooks, *sommeliers* and other staff that could be found anywhere in Italy. This faithful band completely transformed the food at the French

Court. Gone were plain meats, cabbage and beans and in their places came *quenelles*, sweetbreads and dishes with truffles. Much of the art of the *pâtissier* which is so great in France today was also brought to that country from Italy at this time, but unfortunately none of this spread to England. Instead the English developed the reserved attitude towards food that many of them hold to this day: that it is fuel and nothing more. By contrast, the French as a nation, even the poorer peasants, ate extremely well in the late 16th century and acquired the interest and enthusiasm for food that they have today.

The early 17th century was a period when boiled meats of all kinds were extremely popular and the reason for this was that both meat and pudding could be boiled in the same pot, thus producing the following three-course dinner: pudding (to take the edge off the appetite) and boiled flesh followed by soup. However, if this is representative of what was being eaten in good Puritan households, elsewhere cooking was more imaginative. A ray of hope is to be found in a manuscript of Sir Theodore Mayerne which was published in 1658, though almost certainly written some years earlier. In this work, which is called *Archimagirus Anglo-Gallicus* or *Excellent and Approved Receipts and Experiments in Cookery*, Sir Theodore gives a number of splendid recipes including 'How to make the best Sawsidges that ever were eat', and how to make *codling cream*. The latter consisted of apples, cooked and peeled, boiled in damask rosewater to which, when reduced, was added a substantial quantity of cream and sugar. After further cooking the dish was served cold. Another of his excellent dishes was *London Pie* which was an enormous pie containing marrow bones, cock sparrows, potatoes, eringo roots, lettuce, chestnuts, dates, oysters, citron rinds, artichokes, egg yolks (hard boiled), lemons, barberries, pepper, nutmeg, cinnamon, cloves and currants. When the pie was baked, the instructions were to 'liquor it with white wine, butter and sugar'. Another sign that imaginative cooking did not entirely die out under the Commonwealth is found in the list of recipes belonging to Mary Fairfax. The collection is dated 1632 and includes details of how to 'bake venison in a good crust' and how to make 'puffe-paste' and pancakes. Almond fritters provide another example of her delicious recipes.

In spite of these flashes of light in the gastronomic gloom of the 17th century, the general standard of cooking in England was very low and even though the Restoration of 1660 removed the grim shadow of Puritanism, people had become so used to dull food that they knew and desired nothing else. Even in the great houses there was little to eat besides great slabs of meat.

In the 18th century which was, above all, the Age of Elegance, gastronomy took a turn for the better in common with most of the other arts. It became the height of fashion in the great houses to boast of having a French chef and a good dinner in Queen Anne's day might very well have contained white fricassee, tongue and cauliflowers, bacon and beans, veal sweetbreads, marrow pasties, venison pasties and orange pudding as well as roast meat and game. Indeed, at one particular dinner described in a book called *The Complete Family Piece* all these dishes were served and many others as well. In the latter part of the century there was also an improvement in the quality of certain ingredients as a result of the efforts of men like 'Turnip' Townshend who found ways of growing superior vegetables, notably turnips, and Robert Bakewell who invented techniques for breeding far better beef-cattle.

The early years of the 19th century were good ones for the cause of gastronomy in this country and among those who fostered it was 'Prinny', later George IV. Indeed it was his great enthusiasm that succeeded in tempting Carême, the French master-chef, to come to England for two years from 1816 to 1818 to cook at the Royal Pavilion at Brighton. Sadly, Carême found both the cooking and the attitude to *haute cuisine* so poor that it was only a personal liking for Prinny that succeeded in keeping him in England even for that time. Nevertheless, things were much better than they had been and it must be remembered that one of the minor, though significant, effects of the French Revolution of 1789 was to send several first-class French chefs running to England. A number of these men began to set up little French restaurants in London and one might have expected that the great restaurants of Britain today would have grown out of them. In fact, largely because of the work of one man, good eating out in Britain began in the London Clubs. The man responsible for this was Alexis Soyer, chef of the Reform Club from 1837 to 1850. His importance was such that *The Globe* was not greatly exaggerating when it said in 1841, 'The impression grows on us that the man of his age is neither Sir Robert Peel, nor Lord John Russell nor even Ibrahim Pasha, but Alexis Soyer'.

Soyer had started his culinary career in Paris and by the age of seventeen, he had already risen to the rank of head chef at a restaurant in the *Boulevard des Italiens*. Five years later he came to England where he worked first for the Duke of Cambridge and then for the Marquis of Waterford and the Duke of Sutherland. The reputation he gained while working in these great households made the Reform Club eager to obtain his services. Soyer was given the opportunity to design the kitchens for the Club and his

3. Alexis Soyer.

4. Soyer in the kitchens of the Reform Club.

work in this field was so excellent that, on their completion, the Club's kitchens were hailed as the finest in Europe. Never before had kitchens been so thoughtfully laid out, nor had such considerations as ventilation ever been taken so seriously. Beyond this, Soyer was a kindly man and did much to improve kitchen conditions so that they ceased to be red-hot infernos where men swore at each other all day long and drank too much.

Soyer's imaginative genius knew no bounds and on one occasion when he was asked to produce the most luxurious and exotic dinner possible with no expense spared, this was the main dish he invented (sadly, a change in the weather prevented the essential ingredients from arriving from Paris so the dish was not actually served): a whole truffle would be taken for each person and a large hole dug in the side into which would be put a plump ortolan covered with a piece of calf's or lamb's caul. These would then be braised in stock to which half a pint of *Lacrima Christi* had been added. After this they would be placed on a dish with a border of force-meat and a *purée* of truffles made from the hollowed-out pieces. A further plump ortolan per person would be served roasted.

Dishes like this could never be forgotten and soon the papers were regularly printing articles about the excellence of the food at the Reform Club. This made the other London Clubs keen to improve their own cuisine and, while none of them ever reached quite the same standard as the Reform, at least while Soyer was there, men were able to eat extremely well at their Clubs in the second half of the century. But the Clubs had one serious limitation: there could be no question of entertaining ladies at them and it was not until nearer the end of the century that this problem was solved by the advent of the first great restaurants England had ever known.

If any one place was responsible for making eating out in mixed company not only respectable but positively fashionable, it was the Savoy Hotel which opened in 1889. It is true that for the first few months the food was rather heavy and dull but then, as a result of lengthy negotiations conducted by Richard D'Oyly Carte, César Ritz was finally persuaded to take on the post of manager and he brought with him the man who was probably the greatest chef in the world at the time, Auguste Escoffier. The Savoy was then in the happy position of having simultaneously the greatest manager and the greatest chef and between them they could offer the very best possible entertainment to their customers. Ritz saw to the décor and ensured that the service was impeccable while Escoffier surpassed the expectations of even the greatest gourmets with his brilliant creations. He was, of course, basically a master of classical French cuisine but he, like Soyer at the Reform, found that a rich clientele always sought new and more exotic dishes. This was just the spur he needed to exercise his inventive talents to the full. He was utterly wedded to his art, perhaps more so than to his wife, whom he very rarely saw. So, when he became engrossed in

5. The Savoy Hotel in 1890.

perfecting a new dish, he was quite happy to stay up for most of the night to get it just right. His working hours lasted from the early morning, when he supervised the preparation of breakfast, until well after midnight and yet he was not a great eater himself, usually having only a little rice and some fruit for his dinner. His fame spread fast and soon no fashionable hostess could resist the idea of entertaining at the Savoy. They vied with each other as to who could give the more exotic and extravagant parties. Ritz was often called upon to create new settings for these great parties and was frequently

6. César Ritz.   7. Auguste Escoffier.

given a budget of several hundred pounds to spend on the decorations and flowers alone. On one occasion he had part of the ground floor of the hotel flooded to create a Venetian setting where guests were served in gondolas. The cost on that occasion was £15 per head. It is hard to calculate what the equivalent of that would be today, but one may be quite certain that in the 1890s it was a fortune to spend on dinner.

Other restaurants were not slow to jump on the band-wagon and soon there were a number of excellent places to eat, as we shall see in the next chapter.

Thus, by the end of the 19th century, the rise of the great restaurant in England was well under way and the timing was perfect. The King who succeeded Victoria in 1901 was a man who adored his food, a man who led his richer fellow-countrymen to take a far greater interest in it than ever before and who ushered in the age of the *bon viveur*.

Chapter 2

THE EDWARDIAN ERA

QUEEN VICTORIA died in 1901 and while her death was universally mourned, it was by no means disastrous for the cause of gastronomy in England. She had never taken a very enthusiastic interest in food – perhaps she had a little of the Puritan within her which made her feel that it was

8. Edward VII.

sinful to make too much fuss about it. Of course she did not actually prevent others from taking an interest in gastronomy, it was just that she did nothing to give it a helping hand herself. However, quite the reverse was true of her successor Edward VII who, both as Prince of Wales and as King, made no secret of his love of good eating and was a source of inspiration to all those in any way connected with the culinary arts.

Even when he was at Oxford University, Edward's love of food was already apparent and his father, Prince Albert, complained in a letter that he preferred good food to mental effort. He was primarily fond of rich food, drink being of far less import- ance. He never drank excessively and

he almost always drank champagne, but in eating good food and in smoking large cigars he knew no moderation except that once a week – on Sunday – he had a plateful of plain roast beef with Yorkshire pudding. His wife was also enthusiastic about good eating, her great favourite dish being crayfish cooked in Chablis. Edward adored grouse, pheasant, and partridges and was particularly fond of snipe and woodcock stuffed with truffles and served with a rich sauce. Another dish associated with him is *Côtelettes de bécassines à la Souvaroff* which consisted of snipe, boned and halved, stuffed with *foie gras* and forcemeat, shaped into small cutlets and grilled in a pig's caul. The *côtelettes* were served with small slices of truffle and Madeira sauce.

Even at the very end of his life he was still able to eat twelve courses regularly at dinner.

All this enthusiasm on the part of the Prince of Wales and later the King could not fail to have its effect on a great many people and, although he ate mostly in private houses, the influence was felt in restaurants too. Indeed it was a very good period for restaurants and one in which they grew both in number and in quality, though almost exclusively in London. It was a period when eating out in restaurants became, as J. B. Priestley has said, 'a habit common enough among the rich and smart or the semi-Bohemians in London'. Let us therefore take a look at London's restaurants at the turn of the century.

We can be certain that there was virtually nothing worth examining outside London at that time and even in London there was little variety in either the style of the restaurants or the food they served. Restaurants could be put into three categories: grand restaurants, not so grand restaurants, and the cosy pub-like variety. Outside these three categories there were just a few with something rather special of their own but for the most part the food was all Anglo-French or English and, while cellars were undoubtedly well stocked, there was an excessive emphasis placed on champagne which was frequently served throughout a meal, especially if there were ladies present.

There were about a dozen restaurants in London which could most appropriately be called Grand Restaurants and they included such names as the Prince's Hall, Romano's, Verrey's, the Savoy, the Trocadero, the Berkeley, the East Room at the Criterion, the Coburg, Claridges, the Café Royal, and the Carlton. We are fortunate in having some excellent accounts of what all these places were like at the time thanks to the effort of an Old-Harrovian *bon viveur* who wrote regular articles about restaurants in the *Pall Mall Gazette*. His name was Lieutenant-Colonel Newnham-Davis and, being a bachelor, he was able to visit all sorts of different places with all sorts of different people. His articles were never damning because he simply did not write about anywhere that he considered to be unworthy of his interest. Nevertheless he was critical at times about small details, so it seems that he must have been a perceptive eater.

The décor of the Grand Restaurants of that period was always much the same; the ceilings would be beautifully ornamented with mouldings which were often picked out in gold on white (except at the Savoy where it was gold on red) and lighting by the turn of the century was always by means of electric chandeliers. There was usually a profusion of mirrors and the

9. The Savoy Hotel Restaurant in 1889.

walls were often covered in richly coloured material to contrast with the paleness of the ceiling. Verrey's walls were a 'suave dark green' while those at the Prince's Hall were brick red picked out with golden *fleurs-de-lis*. Potted plants were also *de rigueur* and a palm court orchestra was almost inescapable. The Trocadero, which was the centrepiece of Mr. Lyon's catering empire, was particularly palatial with its veined marble entrance and its elegant frieze. Inside, the hand-painted ceiling-panels depicted sporting cupids and the wall-panels were adorned with brocades and silks. A fine orchestra played up in the gilded gallery.

In these splendid settings the cream of London society settled down nightly to enjoy themselves but one cannot help wondering if the whole business did not become a little monotonous, for it was not only the décor which was always much the same. The food varied very little from one Grand Restaurant to another and the emphasis on champagne meant that there was little variety in the drinking, though undoubtedly a few of the connoisseurs would have found an occasional bottle of Perrier-Jouet a pleasant change from the Veuve Clicquot which was the most popular of all champagnes at that time. The structure of the menu scarcely ever varied: there would be a cold *hors-d'œuvre* to begin with and caviare was the great favourite for this course. This would be followed almost always by turtle soup or bortsch – Newnham-Davis at times despaired of ever being able to avoid these two! Occasionally a cream soup was offered as well, but certainly the smart thing to choose was turtle. This would then be followed by the fish course and here again the choice varied very little: it was almost inevitably a fillet of sole in a cream sauce or fried whitebait. When the appetite had been suitably whetted by these preliminaries, the first of the two meat courses would be served. This was usually a rather plain dish of beef or lamb followed by some game or poultry. Here there was much more variety, especially in the second of these courses. The Hotel Cecil offered *Caneton de Rouen à la Presse*; Claridges went in for *Bécassines flambées Empire* and at the Carlton, where the great Escoffier was chef after leaving the Savoy, the *Ortolans au Champagne* were exquisite. The *Aiguillettes de Caneton à l'Orange* at Verrey's and the *Cailles à la Sainte Alliance* at the Criterion were also splendid. The latter dish, which shows the influence of Alexis Soyer, consisted of an ortolan stuffed with truffles embedded in a quail.

Puddings were limited in scope, the most popular choice in the Grand Restaurants being some sort of ice-cream *bombe*. Whether or not this was because even the great Edwardian *bon viveurs* could not face an elaborate pudding after all that had gone before, I do not know, but certainly the food enthusiast of today would be disappointed to find such a limited choice at a highly recommended restaurant. Nevertheless *soufflés* and *crêpes flambées* did occasionally feature on menus. Cheese was rarely served and savouries were, as they are today, an occasional addition to a good dinner. However, no one would have dared to end a meal without serving *friandises*. After-dinner drinking was very much as it is now except that Madeira was then far more popular.

Although the menus I have described were typical of the Grand Restaurants, there were a few places which could offer more exotic things. British officers often returned from India with a taste for curry and this caused the Savoy to employ an Indian sous-chef so that this dish could be as authentically prepared as was possible in England. The Hotel Cecil was also praised for its curry, while the presence of a Russian sous-chef at the Tivoli ensured that the *Zakouski* was good. Furthermore the presence of a great many Americans at the Savoy did not fail to have some influence on the cooking there, so that such dishes as clam chowder and pecan pie began to feature from time to time on the menu.

The second category of restaurants, that is to say the medium-grand ones, were often well worth visiting and they included Simpson's, Rule's, the Cavour, Willis's Rooms, Frascati's, Scott's and Kettner's. Some of these restaurants offered food that was very similar to that served in the Grand Restaurants while others, such as Simpson's, Scott's and Rules, were deliberately and unashamedly simple. The décor and size of these restaurants varied far more than did those of the Grand Restaurants. Some, such as the Holborn, whose grand saloon had three galleries supported by marble pillars and whose entrance-hall was built in multicoloured marble, were on a very splendid scale but their clientele and their slightly lower standard of cooking gave the game away. It was significant that instead of taking a Princess or a famous American heiress to such places, Newnham-Davis usually chose a poor clergyman or one of his theatrical friends as his companion. One of the few restaurants in this category that set out to try and provide some sort of continental atmosphere was Willis's Rooms in King Street which was quite an authentic reproduction of a Parisian restaurant; little scarlet sofas stood by the walls and the wine-waiter was dressed in a proper *sommelier*'s black leather apron. The clientele there was quite smart and it was not uncommon to see an occasional *grande dame* or high-powered financier from the Stock Exchange. The food was good and included such items as *Barbue au vin de Bourgogne* and a slightly more interesting pudding than the eternal *bombe*: *fraises à l'Orange*. But the bill for a good dinner at Willis's Rooms could be very nearly as high as one at a full-scale Grand Restaurant. In the Lieutenant-Colonel's case, dinner for two at Willis's without champagne cost £1·70*, while the price of a comparable dinner at Verrey's, allowing for the extra 35p that champagne cost above the price of claret, was only 5p more.

Unlike Willis's Rooms, Simpson's, Rule's and Scott's all specialized in plain English cooking. Rule's was the oldest of the three and has some claim to be the oldest restaurant in London. It was founded in 1798 by Thomas Rule as an Oysteria and though by Edwardian times it had become a restaurant rather than an oyster bar, it still displayed in its windows two giant shells to which a very remarkable history is attached. According to *The Sunday Times* of 22 November 1868, Mr. Rule was at one time bathing off an island in the China Seas when 'he observed the great oyster of Syngapore (*Tridacna gigas* of Linnaeus) swimming towards him with open jaws. With great presence of mind, he unwound his neckerchief and threw it into the

10. Rule's Restaurant today. The décor still retains its Edwardian character.

*For the sake of clarity, prices throughout the book are expressed in decimal currency.

creature's jaws which immediately shut fast upon it like a vice. He then quietly towed the monster ashore, lit a fire beneath it and cooked it. It afforded ample food for fourteen people for six weeks. At the end of that time, the shells were floated by means of life-belts and Mr. Rule and his friends once more set sail for England.'

The décor of the restaurant consisted of a large number of pictures, prints, and drawings which covered almost every inch of the walls and in this setting a mixture of authors, playwrights, actors, artists, and critics would regularly gather to enjoy a variety of English dishes, especially fish.

Simpson's was grander than Rule's or Scott's having imitation marble columns and trees in tubs, but its prices were very reasonable. A dinner from the joint was to be had for 12½p, while a fish dinner was also offered at 14p. Simpson's was also the largest of the three; it had a separate men's dining-room on the ground floor and a ladies' dining-room upstairs. A good lunch complete with wine cost barely 35p per person. Scott's, like Rule's, specialized in fish and its windows in the Haymarket always displayed fine-looking smoked salmon and lobsters. Inside it also had mock-marble pillars and gave its customers the choice between eating in the cosy 'dive' below or upstairs in the restaurant or grill room. Scott's was just the place for simple but good fish dishes and specialized in lobsters and oysters.

For people who wanted to eat top class food in more modest surroundings and at lower prices the Cavour in Leicester Square was probably the ideal choice and it was particularly popular among actors and actresses who wanted to have an early meal before going on stage. No one ever bothered to put on evening dress at the Cavour unless they were going on to the theatre and high standards were consistently maintained by the *patron* M. Philippe. He could not have had much sleep for he was up by 5 a.m. every day to buy supplies for his restaurant.

Frascati's in Oxford Street was a restaurant of comparable quality but, since its clientele mainly comprised City gentlemen and their wives, it did not share the slightly Bohemian atmosphere of the Cavour. However, its décor was equal to some of the best in London and anyone who was not familiar with the greatest of the London restaurants would undoubtedly have thought, as he entered to the strains of a string orchestra playing and saw the gilt pillars with silver angels at their capitals, that he had reached the ultimate in eating out.

Kettner's is also well worth mentioning for it is one of the few restaurants, apart from hotel restaurants, that in common with such places as Simpson's and Rule's, has survived to this day. It was a snug little place and popular

11. Simpson's in the Strand. The Ladies' dining-room in 1905.

for smaller dinner-parties as it had some very cosy little private dining-rooms. The cooking was of the usual Anglo-French variety.

Another restaurant that is still with us is the Etoile in Charlotte Street and the private rooms there were famous. Equipped with folding-down beds, they were particularly suitable for a man having a naughty night out with his mistress or girlfriend. It is amusing to reflect on this when one considers how very respectable the Etoile is today!

Although, as I have said, the majority of restaurants offered a very similar selection of dishes, there were, of course, a few places which went in for continental specialities. Jewish cooking was to be found at such places as Goldstein's in Blomfield Street which was fully approved by the leaders of the Jewish community. Its food was quite unlike any other restaurant and its dishes included 'Solomon Grundy' which was a form of pickled herring, pease and beans soup and carp stewed in a strong brown sauce made of fish-stock, onions, ginger, and treacle. The sweets included Kugel – a rich mixture of fruits and candies with a thin crust, and almond pudding.

Many people think that the present interest in health-foods is a new phenomenon but this is not so, for even in the 1890s London was not without its vegetarian restaurants, such as the St. George's Café in St. Martin's Lane. Here amid the potted palms, a strange clientele of hypochondriac ladies, a few nuns and ordinary citizens congregated to enjoy such delights as grilled mushrooms with seakale cream or Yorkshire pudding with sage and onions and new potatoes, the latter dish costing 3p. Soups of all suitable sorts, vegetable pies, omelettes, and cheeses were also specialities of the house. Those customers visiting the St. George's for the first time would doubtless have found the wine list novel, for instead of a choice of champagne, claret or burgundy, the vegetarian was invited to have elderberry wine, blackcurrant wine or even ginger-beer.

Many people also believe that before the advent of Wimpy Bars and Golden Eggs there was nowhere for poorer people to go and eat, but this certainly was not true in London. Anyone with even a moderate income could afford to eat at such places as the Restaurant des Gourmets off Leicester Square with its cosy French atmosphere. Here a portion of *pâté* or a bowl of soup cost 1p, an omelette 2p, and the most expensive item on the menu, turbot with caper sauce, cost 3p. The clientele included musicians from neighbouring theatres and coachmen, as well as numerous impoverished Frenchmen. Other comparable places included the Cheshire Cheese in Fleet Street which, of course, still flourishes and the Blue Posts in Cork Street. The Cheshire Cheese was a little more expensive than the Restaurant des Gourmets with the rump steak pudding, which was its speciality, costing 10p, and a further 1p for vegetables. However, this was not unreasonable when one considers that a second helping was always available free of charge. Another popular item at the Cheshire Cheese was stewed cheese – a form of Welsh Rarebit consisting of a portion of cheese mixed with mustard, baked in the oven and served with toast. This delicacy cost 2p.

So far, in examining London restaurants at the beginning of the Edwardian era I have deliberately missed out two establishments because their remarkable history demands that they should be given a place of their own. The two places I have in mind are the Café Royal and the Cavendish Hotel.

The Café Royal was founded by Daniel Nicolas Thevenon (known as Daniel Nicols) who, through no fault of his own, was on the run from the French police. In 1865, fifteen months after arriving in London with just £5 in his pocket, he opened a café in Glasshouse Street called the Café Restaurant Nicols. Such was its success that two years later he bought a large tailor's shop at No. 68 Regent Street – still its postal address – and there opened the Café Royal. The story of how it came to have the famous Napoleonic 'N' as its symbol is worth repeating. Nicols was a devoted Royalist but his son-in-law, Georges Pigache, was an equally ardent Bonapartist. Pigache persuaded Nicols that the 'N' stood for the *Patron*'s name – Nicols – and that the crown above it was simply there to represent the 'Royal' in 'Café Royal'. The fact that it was an imperial crown evidently escaped Nicols' notice.

Soon after opening the Café Royal, Nicols felt that he ought to set about building up a really excellent cellar there. Accordingly he sent to Burgundy for his cousin, Eugène Delacoste, whose taste in wine was unsurpassed. Delacoste was delighted to accept this call for help and began assembling a truly astonishing cellar. The only trouble was that although he undoubtedly bought well and wisely, he spent so much money in so doing that the Café would certainly have gone bankrupt if Mme Nicols had not been able to produce £60,000 out of the blue, money that she had managed to save up unknown to her husband. To give some idea of the scale of the buying, one-eighth of the stock of wine was sold off to help this financial crisis and realized £115,000. No wonder that great *bon viveur* and rake, Frank Harris, said: 'Even in 1884–5 the Café Royal had the best cellar in the world. Fifteen years later it was the best ever seen on earth.'

During the nineties the Café became very popular among the 'arty' circles and its *habitués* included Frank Harris, Oscar Wilde, Lord Alfred Douglas, James McNeill Whistler, Sir Max Beerbohm, and Augustus John.

12. The Café Royal bedecked for the Coronation of Edward VII.

13. Daniel Nicols,
the founder of the Café Royal.

In spite of the presence of this Bohemian clientele in the Domino Room, other parts of the Café were considered to be completely respectable. Indeed, the good Lieutenant-Colonel chose to eat there when he wanted to entertain his niece, who was the highly respectable daughter of a dean. His menu on that occasion in 1898 shows that the food was good enough to compliment the outstanding cellar:

Hors-d'œuvre Russe
Pot-au-feu
Sole Walewska
Noisette d'agneau Lavallière
Haricots Verts à l'Anglaise
Parfait de foie gras
Salade
Pole Nord

The *Sole Walewska* was particularly delicious with its delicate cheesy flavour and the *Pole Nord* was an admirable creation consisting of a *semifreddo* ice-cream inside ordinary ice-cream all set on a pedestal of ice in the shape of a bird nesting on rocks.

Daniel Nicols died in 1897 but the restaurant continued throughout the Edwardian era and well beyond under the highly competent guidance of his widow.

Although founded long before the turn of the century, the Cavendish Hotel in Jermyn Street did not become famous until 1902 and the reason why it is possible to date its fame so precisely is that that was the year in which it was bought by Rosa Lewis – a remarkable lady whose skill as a cook was anxiously sought by anyone who contemplated entertaining a member of the Royal Family. Rosa had begun life as a maid and while working in this capacity used such moments of leisure as she was allowed to read newspaper reports about society functions, balls, banquets and so on. This made her determined to become in some way involved with this world

14. Rosa Lewis.

and she intelligently realized that the best way to do so was by becoming a good cook. This was very sound thinking, for as Rosa's biographer, Daphne Fielding, says: 'Food had never been so important in Society as it was with the Edwardians. People could climb into Society on the shoulders of a good cook.'* Rosa therefore handed in her notice and took on the post of under kitchen-maid in the Comtesse de Paris's house at Mortlake. Although her work at first consisted of scrubbing floors, being a shrewd observer she soon began to absorb a great deal of very valuable information. Much of her gastronomic French vocabulary was gathered here, and as she was found to be both keen and competent she was gradually given more and more important tasks to perform. It was while working for the Comtesse that she first came to know the Prince of Wales who was often entertained there. Later she worked for the Comte de Paris when he had shooting parties in Scotland and this gave the the opportunity to learn about the cooking of game which was to be one of her specialities.

Her talents were given wider scope when she left the Comtesse de Paris and began to be a sort of freelance cook, her services being frequently required by Lady Randolph Churchill. Her culinary education was completed by working for a Mr. William Low of Charleston, Carolina, who was a friend of the Prince of Wales and who employed a coloured cook called Mosianna. Mosianna gave Rosa some valuable instruction in the cooking of the American Deep South, while her great friendship with Auguste Escoffier was also very valuable. Indeed, the great chef called her 'Queen of Cooks' and she claimed that he had taught her more than anyone else.

*Daphne Fielding, *Duchess of Jermyn Street*, (Eyre, 1964).

Rosa decided from the start that she did not wish her hotel to be available to just anyone; all through her life at the Cavendish if anyone irritated her she would often say something like 'You are treating my house like an hotel'. She therefore decided that at first there should be no public dining-room and that, instead, every suite should have its own private dining-room supplied from the hotel kitchen. The prestige of the hotel was greatly enhanced when word got round that one suite was permanently reserved for the King, who visited the hotel incognito at regular intervals so that he and his friends could enjoy Rosa's cooking. In fact it was not as difficult as it may seem for even the King to dine there incognito as Rosa was a master of discretion and was very good at seeing that no unwanted caller ever bothered her guests or even found out that they were there.

The combination of the exquisite cooking, the celebrated *habitués* who, apart from the King, included a great many of those who were in some way associated with the Court, and the fact that Rosa's discretion could be relied upon, all made the Cavendish one of the greatest eating-places of the Edwardian era. The success of the hotel under Rosa's management enabled her to enlarge it and after a few years she decided to have a public dining-room in addition to the private ones. The food there was just as good as in the private rooms and this menu of 26 June 1908 was typical of the daily *table d'hôte*:

Consommé aux Ailerons
Truite froide à la Cavendish
Blanchailles
Soufflé de Cailles à la Valencienne
Pièce de Bœuf à la Gelée en Bellevue
Jambon de Prague aux fèves
Poularde froide à la Parisienne
Salade
Asperges en branches
Pêches au Marron
Bombe glacée Dame Blanche
Friandises
Laitances à la diable

The menu, of course, included a quail dish – no menu of Rosa's would have been complete without one as it was her favourite meat and she was particularly famous for her quail pie.

It was in 1906, four years after Rosa Lewis acquired the Cavendish, that the Ritz Hotel first opened its doors to the public and of all the establishments that opened during Edward's reign none was more illustrious than this.

The Ritz was the third hotel in London to benefit from César Ritz's organizing ability and excellent good taste. Its décor was of the Louis XVI style but the restaurant, unlike so many of the other Grand Restaurants in London, was decorated in delicate pastel shades. There were no violent colours and heavily gilded areas here; instead it was adorned with pastel-shaded marble and was painted cream, rose, and soft green. The floor was covered with a fine Aubusson carpet and all the furniture was in period.

As was to be expected at any establishment connected with M. Ritz, the hotel and restaurant were immediately adopted by the highest level of society and the German and Austrian embassies even went so far as to retain a table for all meals. The restaurant was under the management of M. Charles and the kitchen under M. Malley who was transferred to London from the Paris Ritz. The kitchens reflected the wider gastronomic horizons of the second half of Edward's reign for, in addition to numerous Frenchmen, it contained a Viennese pastry cook and an expert in Russian soups. The cakes at the Ritz were so outstanding that the King, finding that his own *pâtissier* could not compete, used to have a regular supply sent to Buckingham Palace.

M. Malley was an inventive chef and such creations as *Saumon Marquise de Sévigné* – salmon with a mousse of crayfish – soon made his reputation in London. Other specialities of the house were *Filet de Sole Romanoff* served with mussels, small slices of apple and artichokes – 'the apple giving a suspicion of bitter sweetness as a contrast to the flesh of the fish' – and *Poulet en Chaudfroid* which was a chicken accompanied by a pink mousse lightly flavoured with curry. Among the *entremets*, M. Malley's greatest creation was probably *Pêche Belle Dijonaise* – a combination of peaches and blackcurrant sorbet with a little *crème de cassis*. In common with all other places associated with the great master after whom it was named, the Ritz also boasted an excellent cellar.

*   *   *

Of course there were changes in the Edwardian era, as in all others. Rosa Lewis commented at the end of the period that hostesses had become far more money-conscious and that, whereas towards the end of the Victorian period three guineas a head did not seem excessive, at the outbreak of the First World War hostesses were unwilling to spend more than one guinea a head. As a result menus tended to become shorter and, in the years that followed, gradually took on the modern shape of three to four courses and no more. But Rosa Lewis pointed out that in order to compensate for the shorter menus, larger portions were called for; that those who had once been content with half a stuffed quail now called for a whole one and those who had once been satisfied with a few slices of truffle now wanted a whole large one.

There were other changes within the restaurant world. The Grand Restaurants continued to flourish but more and more restaurants serving different types of foreign food began to appear. Newnham-Davis felt that by the end of the period it was no longer necessary to leave London at all in order to enjoy the gastronomic pleasures of foreign travel. Another trend was the increased popularity of grill rooms. Life was becoming more hectic and Americans were exerting their influence on London and both these factors helped to bring grill rooms into favour.

The first decade of this century saw the arrival of a great many Italian *restaurateurs* and waiters in England and, while some of them chose to open restaurants that served the usual kind of Anglo-French cooking, some were brave enough to offer exclusively Italian dishes and many offered Italian wines, especially *Asti Spumante* which Edwardian ladies found a delightful change from the constant flow of champagne, while their escorts were pleased to find that it put their bank balance under far less strain than when they ordered the produce of Rheims and Epernay.

At the Florence in Rupert Street, for example, it was perfectly possible to dine on *antipasto assortito*, *ravioli*, *scallopine di vitello alla Milanese* and *zabaglione* with *Asti*, *Chianti*, and *Barolo* to accompany it. Nor was this exceptional, for Soho was already beginning to have a considerable number of little Italian restaurants by 1914 and they all seemed to do well. Most of them were of the cheaper variety, offering a *table d'hôte* at about 12½p and Pinoli's in Wardour Street offered an excellent menu at only 10p. At another Italian-run restaurant, the Ship in Whitehall, a good set lunch was offered for only 3½p. But some of these Italian places were extremely good and quite grand; a good example was the old-established Pagani's in Great Portland Street. This restaurant had been opened in the 1870s by Mario Pagani chiefly to cater for a poorer clientele of journalists, artists and singers all seeking something a little adventurous and colourful. His Italian cooking had gone down very well and he made so much money that the restaurant increased in both size and grandeur. At the end of the century the management raised the tone further by offering a selection of French dishes. Nevertheless, even at the end of the period *minestrone, spaghetti, macaroni, gnocchi,* and *fritto misto* could still be eaten there in very civilized surroundings. The main private dining-room at Pagani's, known as the Artists' room, was particularly famous because the walls were covered with celebrities' signatures, sketches and caricatures.

In describing the restaurants of London at the beginning of the Edwardian period I have had to complain about the lack of genuine 'Frenchness' in the so-called French restaurants, Willis's Rooms being the only exception. However, by the end of the period there were a number of more genuine French restaurants of which a good example was Gustaves' in Greek Street. Here the clientele was predominantly French and the décor had no pretentions; the walls were cream and chocolate and the floor was covered in oilcloth. In these surroundings diners could enjoy *escargots, soupe à l'oignon, moules marinières* and *râble de lièvre* and almost forget that they were still in London.

Another important innovation in the London gastronomic scene was the advent of the first Chinese restaurant, the Cathay, which opened in Piccadilly Circus in 1908. Far from being the modern type of cheap and simple Chinese restaurant, the Cathay was, and still is, a grand establishment, but although its décor might have been more subject to French than Oriental influence, in so much as the wallpaper had a pattern of gold *fleurs-de-lis*, the cooking, which was all supervised by a Chinese chef and served under the watchful eye of a Chinese manager, was all quite authentic. The clientele was made up of Chinese, and English people who had at one time or another visited the Far East. Other diners were people who had not travelled outside Europe but who wanted to enjoy a novel gastronomic experience. There is no need to go into detail about the menu as almost all the dishes we expect to find in Chinese restaurants today were to be found at the Cathay long before the First World War, and probably more authentically cooked too. However, it is interesting to note that there were a few dishes that were quite out of the ordinary, including sliced jelly-fish with pickle.

Another national cuisine which was beginning to make its mark in London by the end of the Edwardian era (just in time to go firmly out of fashion for political reasons), was German food, and probably the best place to sample this was at Appenrodt's in Coventry Street. Herr Appenrodt had started by building up a little chain of German delicatessen shops in London before opening his restaurant, and although he had a staff of various nationalities, including a French chef, there were enough Germans on the staff to ensure that all examples of their national cooking offered to their customers were authentic. Appenrodt's restaurant must have been one of the very first gastronomic casualties of the First World War, of which we shall hear more later.

The final important trend in Edwardian eating out was, as I have said, the increased popularity of grill rooms which were, arguably, the fore-runners of the modern steak-house. As far as one can see, the grill room came into existence towards the end of the 19th century, when large numbers of American visitors began to appear in London. Often these Americans were unwilling to change into white tie and tails for dinner, yet, at the same time, they did not wish to impose themselves in informal dress upon the diners in smart restaurants. Many hotels and restaurants therefore came up with the idea of having a grill room in addition to a dining-room in which good but more simple food would be served to informally dressed diners and in which a dinner could be very speedily served to those who had to eat in a hurry. The idea went from strength to strength in the early years of this century as more and more hard working businessmen and others found that, after an exhausting day at the office, it was far more relaxing to slip out to a grill room than to stagger into their tail-suits. Other people caught on to the idea and soon grill rooms had a substantial following among those who wanted to eat well but with a minimum of fuss.

One of the very first grill rooms was to be found at the *old* Savoy Hotel but, although it was excellent, it did not become very well known. The policy in such places was to serve the usual range of grilled chops and steaks together with one or two hot made-up dishes, but the choice of these was always very limited. A few simple first courses, usually cold, ice-cream and cheese completed the bill of fare. When the *new* Savoy opened in 1889 it was, of course, equipped with a grill room which was called the Café Parisien. Here it was apparently possible for the tardy theatregoer to gobble down a four course dinner in barely half an hour with a minimal risk of indigestion, though many people wisely preferred to linger over their meal. The décor of these grill rooms was always more simple than that of their sister restaurants and so at the Prince's Hall, where the restaurant was, as we have seen, highly ornate and elegant, the grill room was a plain white room with panelled walls and dark leather armchairs. Even at the Troca-dero, where the décor of the grill room was more exotic than elsewhere, the walls of grey marble, gold, and buff were no match for the Restaurant. Only at the Café Royal was the grill room as splendid as a grand restaurant and it was said that the best *entrecôtes* in London were to be found there. The grill room at the Carlton Hotel, however, was far more conventional, being decorated in white apart from the blue china on the shelves.

Romano's Restaurant decided that it also needed a grill room but that it should have a touch of originality. Accordingly, they turned the old kitchen into a reproduction Russian farmhouse and dressed the waiters in white blouses with red sashes. The great advantage of eating there was that many of the dishes from the main restaurant were available at a far more moderate price. And what dishes they were! The chef, M. Ferrario, was one of the most broadminded in London and, in addition to the usual Anglo-French range of dishes which he cooked splendidly, he was able to offer anything from Nigerian ground-nut soup to *moussaka* and Malay curry. Even his English dishes were out of the ordinary and there were not many other good restaurants where the winter menu included Lancashire hot-pot and gipsy pot.

*   *   *

Although Edward VII died in 1910, the spirit of his reign continued for a few more years in spite of the fact that his successor, George V, was by no stretch of the imagination a *bon viveur*. Something of his gastronomic inclinations can be learned from the fact that, after his trip to India in 1912, he gave standing orders to the kitchen staff at the Palace to serve some sort of curry at every meal to which no important guests had been invited. However, by 1913, although the pace was not slackening, there were beginning to be a few blots on the horizon. The Waldorf Hotel little knew how near to the truth it was coming when, at its New Year's Eve Dance in 1912, the following scene was enacted:

Father Time wheeled in a submarine marked 1913 which began to bombard an old ship marked 1912. As the clock struck twelve, the old ship began to sink while the lights in the room were extinguished, leaving only the submarine's searchlights to illuminate the spectacle. All this was prophetic because, although the First World War did not, of course, break out until the following year, 1913 was really the last year of Edwardian life; it was the swansong and, after it had passed, life in England was never the same again. It was as though the whole way of life had sunk like that old ship, to live on only in people's memories.

Already by 1913 the servant problem was beginning to be felt. This did not apply to the grand houses which kept a substantial staff but it did apply to middle class homes where the family wanted to employ a cook-general, in other words someone to cook for the family and help in other ways about the house. In many cases it was found necessary to pay £26 per year to obtain the services of such a person!

15. The Waldorf Hotel in 1914.

The growing difficulty of obtaining staff after the First World War was one of the factors which led more members of the middle classes to begin going to restaurants.

The outbreak of the First World War dealt gastronomy a devastating blow. England was not at all prepared for the food shortages which the war was bound to bring. British agriculture only provided a small fraction of the nation's food supplies in 1914; for instance, four out of every five slices of bread eaten were made of foreign wheat and three out of five slices were spread with imported butter. Four-fifths of the lard requirement was imported, two-thirds of the ham and bacon and three-quarters of the cheese. To be technical for a moment, we produced only 35 per cent of the calories we consumed and this naturally made us very vulnerable to attacks on our shipping. This was particularly felt after February 1915 when Germany declared the waters round Britain a 'war zone' which both enemy and neutral ships entered at their own risk. However, we were fortunate in having a breathing space as U-boat activity did not become severe until January 1917 and this gave time to set up a rationing system and introduce other controls. This was just as well for, in the first six months of 1917, 3,856,998 tons of shipping were lost and food imports were thus very drastically cut. The situation did improve after that with the introduction of the convoy system but everything remained in short supply for the whole of the rest of the war.

To try and improve the supply situation the Government gave itself, late in 1916, almost unlimited powers to control the distribution of food and at the same time ordered that 'war bread' should be introduced – that is bread made by extracting a higher percentage of flour from the grain than normal. The Savoy Restaurant tried to give some further help to the bread situation by displaying this notice on all tables in the spring of 1917:

In view of Lord Devonport's warning
and the increased shipping losses
MANY VISITORS MAY WISH TO ABSTAIN FROM BREAD
at luncheon and dinner.

To meet the wishes of such visitors
Polenta (maize meal) and rice cake, both
of which are sufficient substitutes,
will be served.

Restaurants were very good about observing the regulations on food. Small wonder then that a number of *restaurateurs* were furious when it was found that the Café Royal was still serving pure white bread some time after the introduction of war bread. Soon the accusations became so vehement that the Café was obliged to face an official investigation at which, in order to avoid prosecution, it was forced to reveal a trade secret; there was no question of breaking the law or of black market dealings – it was simply that an extremely clever *pâtissier* at the Café had discovered a way to make excellent white flour out of potatoes!

In June 1917 sugar rationing was introduced, after which each person was only allowed ½ lb per week and then, early in 1918, meat, butter, and lard were also rationed. The latter piece of legislation prompted Captain Nicols Pigache to say in his own book* on the Café Royal:

> The exigencies of the war made it extremely difficult to obtain anything approaching the ingredients and the qualities required for the very best cooking. The day that the Café Royal had to tumble from its high estate and succumb to a mixture of margarine and butter was too dreadful for words.

In the Savoy, as a waiter there, Filippo Ferraro recalled,† 'We substituted vegetables for meat, corn-meal for wheat, margarine for butter and saccharine for sugar.'

But supply shortages were by no means the only problem that restaurants had to face during the war. Shortages of customers and staff were equally serious for, very soon after the war began, all the major restaurants found that their customers were enlisting in large numbers and going off to the Front, in many cases never to return. English staff enlisted in large numbers while foreign staff left to join their native armies if they were on the right side or were interned if they were on the wrong side.

Immediately, many of the German-run restaurants in Soho displayed large signs saying 'under new Swiss management', while a number of German waiters at the Café Royal stood on tables and sang the Marseillaise. But it was all to no avail as the authorities were very thorough in rounding up German nationals.

The effect of all this has been vividly described in Stanley Jackson's‡ book on the Savoy:

* Nicols Pigache, *Café Royal Days* (Hutchinson, 1934).
† F. Ferraro, *From Candlelight to Flashlight* (Falcon Press, 1952).
‡ Stanley Jackson, *Savoy* (Frederick Muller, 1964).

In the huge, half-empty kitchen with a skeleton staff of clumsy boys and tired old men, the maître-chef cursed the Boche and tried somehow to camouflage his rissoles.

At the Cavendish Hotel, in order to be able to keep the kitchen going, Rosa Lewis had to ask the wives of Guards officers staying in the hotel to help with all the household chores.

Amateur service and inferior ingredients were the least of the hazards facing those who dined out in London restaurants during this difficult period – a far graver hazard came from air-raids. After a while a number of the larger places began to close earlier than usual for safety though, even so, quite a number of people were killed or injured in restaurants before the war ended. One of those who suffered (but lived on in perfect health to tell the tale) was Ferraro, who has left this account of his experiences of First World War air-raids:

> We nearly forgot that there was a war until the visits of Fokkers began to terrorize the citizenry – sometimes five or six of these dreadful invaders would come at once. On the whole the guests carried on cheerfully, even when the bombs exploded so near that it seemed as though the next would fall on top of the Café Parisien (Savoy Grill) itself. This nearly happened . . . I was standing with my friend Désiré, now a wine-butler at the Savoy, at a window overlooking the old BBC headquarters on Savoy Hill, and the din of the bombing seemed to come so close that I said to him 'We had better move, it is getting too near for my liking'. We had both walked a few steps when there was a deafening crash, and we found ourselves in the grill room without knowing how we had got down the short staircase. The whole corner of a block of houses was blown up and the impact of the giant explosion had blasted my friend and me to safety. . . .

> On another occasion while sipping coffee one night in Lyons Corner House near Piccadilly Circus, four of us were in a jolly mood with Alletto, once manager of the Ritz Restaurant, as chief fun-maker.

> Our best joke was the banging of the service door in the large café whenever the waitress brought in fresh supplies. Alletto compared this noise to the bombs of war and no sooner had he mentioned the word Zeppelin than we heard a strange and startling sound, followed by a tremendous crash which really heralded the first visit of the German monsters to England. Everyone rushed to the doors of the restaurant . . .

a young sailor struck an heroic pose and shouted 'Women and children first'. The burly Swiss superintendent, mindful of his duties spread-eagled himself against the main exit, crying: 'Please! bills to be paid first' and so prevented an unprofitable exodus of customers.

At last, in November 1918, the Armistice was signed and the restaurants gradually came back to life again. But no one could deny that major changes had occurred during the war years and that the 'normal life' to which the restaurants returned late in 1918 was a new one, devoid of almost all the hall-marks of the Edwardian period.

Chapter 3

THE INTER-WAR YEARS

ALTHOUGH restaurants recovered considerably more quickly from the First World War than from the Second, there was no question of an instant recovery, and as late as 1929 André Simon wrote:

> We are, happily, approaching the stage when the art of good living is again receiving proper attention. Today, barely ten years after the Great War, we are not yet back to the pre-war level but on our way there.

In fact, many of the restrictions imposed on restaurants during the war remained in force until 1921, and so it was only then that any significant improvement could get under way. 1921 was also the year of an extremely important piece of legislation: a licensing act which permitted drinks to be ordered after 11 p.m. provided that a sandwich, or other food, was ordered with them. But the restaurants were certainly changed, and so were people's requirements. John Burnett commented in his book *Plenty and Want*:*

> The dietary standards of the wealthier classes declined somewhat between the wars. This was partly a consequence of choice and partly of necessity. The taste for the solid, endless repasts of Victorian days were changing in favour of shorter, lighter meals, more suited to the accelerated pace of life and better adapted to the new knowledge of nutrition which was beginning to influence people's tastes.

An example of this change in eating habits is the State Banquet held in honour of President Hoover in 1919, which consisted of ten courses. Until this time no state banquet had ever comprised fewer than fourteen. Equally, the wedding breakfast of the Duke and Duchess of York, held in 1923, consisted of only eight courses.

Herbedeau, the great master-chef of Ritz and Carlton fame, commented in the mid-1920s that: 'Undoubtedly customers do eat less now than in bygone years. In the first place cocktails are responsible, for, contrary to belief, they kill an appetite, and secondly, nobody wishes to become fat.'

Perhaps for many people the smaller quantities of food served were to some extent compensated for by the various forms of entertainment which became popular in restaurants after the war. Perhaps it was by way of

* *Plenty and Want* (Nelson, 1966).

reaction to the gloomy and deprived war years that people now called for dancing and cabaret in all the major restaurants. When Pepino Leoni, who later founded the Quo Vadis restaurant in Soho, returned to England after the war he commented, 'I came back to a London very different from the one I had left in 1915. It was a gay London, casting from its mind the dark years of war, eager to enjoy itself.' One of those quickest to see what was wanted was George Reeves-Smith of the Savoy. The idea of interrupting a fine meal with comic acts and songs from the stage must have secretly appalled him, but he nevertheless realized that it was absolutely essential to offer a good cabaret if the Savoy was to remain among the foremost restaurants in London. Accordingly, at enormous expense, he had hydraulic jacks installed to raise the Savoy's 400 square yards of dance floor by 27 inches and thus make it into a stage when required. He also ensured that the hotel employed the very best cabaret acts available. Many of the other leading restaurants quickly followed the Savoy's lead, and those which could not afford a cabaret at least tried to provide the best possible band for dancing.

The years following the end of the war saw the appearance of a number of new restaurants as well as the revival of some older ones. Undoubtedly the first good new restaurant to open in that period was the Ivy in Seven Dials. Its founder, Mr. Abel, had had the courage to open even before the war clouds had vanished. His policy was to create a good restaurant but one that at the same time was in some ways quite modest. The success of his policy was quickly proven, because, in spite of the fact that no flowers adorned the tables and the décor was predominantly brown, he never had the slightest difficulty in filling the restaurant with crowds of famous writers, actors, and actresses. Its complete lack of ostentation gave it a snug and almost club-like atmosphere. The modesty of the décor and the absence of music was not entirely reflected in the prices, which were high, but the food was of a high enough standard to justify this. The specialities included *Suprême de Sole Maison*, *Poussin en Cocotte Polonaise*, and some exquisite ice-cream *bombes*.

Another agreeable addition to the London restaurant world after the First World War was the Maison Basque in Dover Street which, with some justification, described itself as *Restaurant Français du Premier Ordre*. It was a restaurant of the *premier ordre* in many senses – a good dinner for two could easily cost over £3, which was a high price to pay, and the exceptional wine list tempted customers to choose rare château-bottled clarets. It also made something of a speciality of Chablis, of which a fine selection was offered.

The cooking did full justice to the cellar, and those who had tasted the Maison Basque's *Cailles Souvaroff*, stuffed and garnished with *foie gras* and truffles and accompanied by a sauce whose ingredients included sherry and *jus lié*, did not quickly forget it.

Au Jardin Des Gourmets perhaps offered better value, for one could eat extremely well there for about £1, and its *patron*, M. Silvy, had learned enough as *maître d'hôtel* at Boulestin to be able to offer superb service. The Jardin had very original décor for the time, the wall being covered with a mural depicting a delightful garden. Such specialities as *Fonds d'artichaut François Villon*, which were served with a succulent cheesy sauce, the *Délices de sole maison* and the *Kebab à l'orientale* soon gave the restaurant a fine reputation.

One of the most agreeable medium-priced restaurants of this time was Le Perroquet in Leicester Square. Decorated in silver and three shades of pink, it provided an *ambiance sympathique* in which to enjoy its cuisine. M. Bellometti, the *chef-patron*, was particularly proud of his *Ris de veau aux pointes d'asperges* and his *suprême de volaille sous cloche* – the latter being the breast and wing of a chicken, floured and fried in batter then finished in wine, brandy, and double cream. Those diners who still had a little room left could enjoy some splendid *entremets* such as *Poire Marie Brizard*.

A most successful post-war revival was made by Kettner's. The restaurant had opened in 1861 and after a number of highly successful years, enjoying the regular patronage of, among others, Edward VII as Prince of Wales, had declined by the end of the Edwardian era. Happily, it was acquired after the war by Arthur Giordano, who had learned the restaurant trade at the Savoy and, by applying his Savoy training to his new acquisition, he quickly raised the tone. He had the whole place redecorated inside and out; the lounges in a Florentine style and the dining-rooms in modern Parisian style and with typical attention to detail, Giordano saw to it that all the flower arrangements were particularly attractive. One dining-room – the largest – had enough space for a dance floor and orchestra. In addition to the usual range of Anglo-French dishes, an Italian speciality *Gnocchi alla Romana*, was always offered. On Sundays they always offered one of their great specialities: *Cannelloni Charlotte Kettner's*.

The Hungaria, which opened in 1928, was in many ways one of the most novel restaurants to appear in the whole of the inter-war period, for never before had there been a first-class, smart restaurant that did not specialize in French, English or Italian cuisine. The Hungaria was, of course, Hungarian, and a spirit of nationalism applied to the food, the wine and the music. Inevitably a certain amount of French food was to be found on the premises, though this was confined to the restaurant. The grill offered a selection of Hungarian dishes such as *Trout à la Tatra*, Hungarian turbot with onion and tomato and Paprika Chicken. The fine selection of national wines was due to the support of the Hungarian Tourist Authority, which regarded the restaurant as a publicity venture.

16. Francis Latry.

It was also during the post-war years that Francis Latry came to fame as *chef de cuisine* at the Savoy Restaurant.

Latry was one of those rare chefs who was both a creative artist and an inventive genius. He always spent his holidays in France at Gex near Lake Geneva and would return with new ideas for dishes at the Savoy. Whether the fact that Gex was only three miles from the birthplace of Brillat-Savarin had any significance, I cannot say, but Latry's menu for the Brillat-Savarin centenary lunch at the Savoy was worthy of that great gourmet, and the dishes included crayfish with *foie gras* and fresh-water fish poached in Burgundy and then charcoal-broiled. At a banquet for great chefs held at the Savoy, he produced golden pheasant stuffed with oysters and tiny grapes from Chablis and *Neige au Clicquot* – a sorbet of cream and 1906 champagne.

Even in the early 1920s, almost any dish, however exotic, could be obtained at the Savoy, among other things: bear's ham from Finland, snails, frogs' legs, and plovers' eggs (at £1·05 each). Strawberries were available out of season at £1·25 per dozen, which in the early twenties must have made them worth their weight in gold!

American tourists were becoming increasingly important to London hoteliers at this time, and so Latry tried to help them feel at home by offering some of their favourite dishes. On Independence Day the menu sometimes read like this:

Washington Melon
Bunkers Hill Soup
Liberty Soles
Maryland Chicken
Independence Salad
Harding Meringue

To make sure that the American food offered at the Savoy was as authentic as possible, the hotel imported turkeys and sweet potatoes from the United States.

Let us now turn from the post-war restaurant scene and look at some of the men who were most closely involved in the post-war revival of good food, for in gastronomy, as in all other fields of civilized life, there is always someone who looms above all competitors as the acknowledged leader in his particular time.

In Britain the leader in the early 19th century was Carême, in the mid-century, Alexis Soyer, and in Edwardian days, Auguste Escoffier. But who should be considered to have succeeded these men during the inter-war years? Two obvious candidates immediately come to mind: Latry of the Savoy and Herbedeau of the Ritz and the Carlton but, much as I admire both of them, when one is seeking to find the person who had the greatest influence on the post-war revival of gastronomy and indeed throughout the whole inter-war period, the award must surely go to one who, in the first instance, was more a journalist and interior decorator than chef: Marcel Boulestin.

Boulestin was first heard of in this country before the First World War as a theatre critic. He then served with the British forces as an interpreter, returning to live in London when the war was over. He set up a shop called 'Modern Decoration' but this was not a tremendous success as numerous little firms of interior decorators were establishing themselves at that time (a number of them run by Society women) and, besides, Boulestin's ideas were too *avant-garde*. At the same time he produced and edited a book of pictures and articles by English and French writers and artists which, although it was well reviewed, sold only a little over 300 copies. All this brought him very near bankruptcy and so he began to give French lessons

17. Marcel Boulestin being televised.

and, to save money, cooked for himself rather than going out to restaurants. He also spent some of his time writing articles for the *Bookman's Journal* and the *Anglo-French Review*, advising people on wines and spirits, importing certain French culinary specialities and cooking for people's dinner parties. As a result of these dinner parties his friends suggested that he should bring out a book of recipes and so Boulestin mentioned the idea to Theodore Byard of Heinemann, who made him sign the contract for *Simple French Cooking for English Homes* on the spot. As he said himself 'I had never learned anything, but I had eaten well all my life, and like the majority of my compatriots of the south-west, I had an instinct for cooking.'

In 1923, Robin Adair came to Boulestin with a letter of introduction from a friend and this was the start of a most valuable and important friendship and partnership. Adair had just arrived in London from Jamaica and was looking for an interesting occupation in London, if possible one connected with either food or music. After the publication of Boulestin's second cookery book, many of his friends urged him to open a restaurant and he agreed to do so with Robin Adair as his partner. A small limited company was formed and Clough Williams-Ellis (of Portmeirion fame) was called in as architect to convert a shop in Leicester Square into the restaurant. Boulestin engaged an excellent chef named Bigorre who had been at the Restaurant Paillard, and his restaurant opened in May 1925. Bigorre made up by his practical experience for what Boulestin and Adair lacked and he was also ready to learn some of Boulestin's original and imaginative dishes, one example of which was the *Omelette Boulestin* – stuffed with mushrooms and fresh cream. The restaurant, which was simply called the 'Restaurant Française', was an instantaneous success and there were numerous reasons for this. Firstly,

Boulestin's books had been widely enough read for his name to have become well known and, secondly, it was almost the only genuine French restaurant in London at the time – most of those that had been French before the war having by that time become Italianized. Nowhere else could offer a Parisian atmosphere and, at a time when good cooking was almost always confined to enormous hotel restaurants, many people must have found this corner of Leicester Square a refreshing and delightful change. Furthermore Boulestin's restaurant was unusual in having an exclusively *à la carte* menu at a time when almost all restaurants of its size only offered *table d'hôte*. Boulestin proved conclusively that his policy of running an authentic French restaurant was absolutely right when, as an experiment, he once offered Devonshire clotted cream and Stilton; not a single customer touched either.

The beef, mutton, cream, and butter were all English, while the vegetables, fruit, cheese, and coffee, were flown in from France. The specialities of the restaurant included the omelette which I have mentioned, game *à la crême*, saddle of hare and *Crêpes Verlaine*. The latter were prepared with a mixture of six liqueurs and some absinthe, but were not served *flambées*.

One of the great problems of this restaurant was that all the drinks – *apéritifs*, wines, and liqueurs, had to be fetched from a near-by pub because Boulestin had no licence and there was no way of obtaining one quickly in those days. This, sadly, meant that no older vintages could be offered because they would inevitably have been shaken up in transit. However, Boulestin used the time while waiting for a licence to build up stocks of well-chosen wines which were kept in storage while he served young wines from the pub. Eventually a wine licence did come through but the problem of fetching spirits from the pub remained, and this was one of the reasons why he listened with some interest when the owners of Sherry's Restaurant in Southampton Street asked him if he would be interested in some sort of collaboration. Boulestin hesitated for a while as Sherry's had not been doing at all well but, in the end, when a shareholders' meeting was called, the advantageous terms put forward, together with the restaurant's proximity to the Royal Opera House, made him decide to accept the offer.

Boulestin commissioned some panels from Laboureur, who had been a fellow interpreter with him during the war, and also some work from Marie Laurencin to adorn the new restaurant and it opened under the name of 'Restaurant Boulestin' in October 1926 (the Leicester Square restaurant having been closed down in August).

The new restaurant accommodated eighty people. Seven chefs, plus a salad-and-coffee maker, prepared the food and, as before, the policy of providing real French cooking was adhered to. Journalists present at the opening were surprised to find coal ranges and charcoal grills in the kitchen instead of new-fangled equipment and modern gadgets, but Boulestin insisted that it was only by using this sort of equipment that really high standards could be maintained. Among his other policies Boulestin insisted that there should be no excessive show or sham – perhaps that was why he did not go in for *crêpes flambées*!

The proximity to the Opera was undoubtedly one of the restaurant's greatest assets and when the season opened with 'The Ring' every table was reserved a fortnight in advance. Boulestin was not at all a believer in cabarets, music or ostentation of any kind but one small exception to this was that he allowed a trumpeter to sound Siegfried's fanfare ten minutes before the end of the opera dinner-interval as a warning to those who did not have a box and therefore had to be sure of getting to their seats on time. On the first occasion when this was done the entire restaurant immediately burst into enthusiastic applause and the trumpeter, who came from the Opera orchestra, afterwards remarked 'It's the first time I've ever been clapped.'

Some of the Leicester Square specialities, such as the omelette and the *crêpes*, came on to Southampton Street but there were also a number of new dishes, such as *Koulibiaca de Saumon, Becasses au Fumet* and an authentic *piperade*.

The restaurant was, of course, an enormous success and it was not long before the list of *habitués* included Lloyd George, the Aga Khan, G. K. Chesterton, Hilaire Belloc, Epstein, Sir John Gielgud, and Virginia Woolf.

Of course Boulestin's success as a *restaurateur* had enormous effect in bringing about the post-war revival in gastronomy, but it was not only in this capacity that his influence was felt. His books on cooking served to whet the appetites of cooks from all levels of society, since many of his dishes did not require particularly expensive ingredients, so that by the late 1930s the English-language editions had sold over 70,000 copies. He also made a series of culinary films for a gas company which were shown in cinemas all over the country and he even recorded for H.M.V. instructions on how to prepare an omelette – complete with the sound of the cooking. The first recording of this disc was wasted because, just as he was saying 'And the omelette white, perfect, slides silently on to the dish', he happened to knock the microphone which transmitted a thunderous sound on to the record. In addition, he gave cookery lessons to a very large number of people over the years – indeed his pupils included a lady-in-waiting to the

18. Restaurant Boulestin.

Queen, an admiral who wanted to be in a position to make constructive comments about the food at his club, and Mrs. Winston Churchill. Obviously this helped to form a generation of Englishmen who really cared about their food and the great man's influence was still further extended when he became the first television chef. Although television served a very much smaller audience in the late 1930s than today, it could be received throughout the greater London area and as far north as Manchester. Between 1937 and 1939 Boulestin appeared twice a month for a quarter of an hour television session. It was a brave thing to take on, as the programme was sent out from a very cramped studio in which the combined effect of the lights and the stove was to generate tremendous heat and, furthermore, Boulestin was asked to move about as little as possible in order not to upset the camera focus. The fact that only a quarter of an hour was allocated and that the programme went out live, inevitably caused serious problems of timing and limited the choice of dishes to those that could be prepared, cooked and served within that time, and so such items as omelettes, *filets de sole au vin blanc, escalopes de veau à la crème, sauce Sabayon, sauce Béarnaise* and *crêpes flambées* were on his list. Disasters were very rare on this programme, the only recorded one being an occasion when Boulestin was cooking a flat omelette which had to be tossed. The camera failed to follow the toss and so, as far as viewers were concerned, the omelette was hurled into the air never to return!

We must now leave Marcel Boulestin and look at some of the other leading figures of the 1920s. But if anyone doubts my claim that he was, in gastronomy, the greatest and most influential man of his age, I would merely refer them to a quotation from *The Times* which described him as 'That most French of Frenchmen who has become almost a British national institution'.

Another figure (whom we have already mentioned) became a legend in his own lifetime. He was Filippo Ferraro, manager of the Berkeley Restaurant from 1922 to 1939. Ferraro was born in Sorrento, where he received an unusual training for one destined to rise to great fame in the restaurant world – he went to art school. This endowed him with a love of painting which continued throughout his life and, in hard times, even helped him out financially when favourite customers bought his paintings.

He first came to England at the age of fifteen when he worked in private service in London. Later he moved to the Carlton Hotel in time for the opening night. He then worked in a variety of hotels abroad, including the Ritz in Paris, the Riviera Palace at Monte Carlo, and the Grand Hotel in

19. Filippo Ferraro.

Rome, before returning to London and working at the Hotel Cecil. Then after a brief time at the Savoy, he went abroad again and became restaurant manager of the Savoy Hotel at Fontainebleau. He was still there in 1914 when suddenly the hotel emptied and he and his staff were left to struggle home and find work. Through the good offices of his brother, who was working in London, Ferraro was able to find employment at the Berkeley Hotel. Three months later, the company transferred him to the Savoy Grill (then called Café Parisien) where he became a *maître d'hôtel*. He worked there throughout the war and in his spare time acted in amateur drama-tic performances to raise money for Italian families in England whose husbands and fathers had been called away to war.

In 1919, when Sovrani became manager of the Savoy Grill (its name was changed in that year) he appointed Ferraro as his second-in-command. For some time everything ran splendidly and, although Sovrani was well known for being difficult to work with, the good-natured and diplomatic Ferraro got on well with him. Only once was there serious trouble; an important customer had been very badly looked after and, although Ferraro had done his best to apologize, the customer had warned him, on leaving, that he would report the matter to the directors. Three days later he received a message that he was to go and see Sir George Reeves-Smith, managing director of the Savoy Group, and it was in a state of considerable anxiety that he knocked on the door of the great man's office. However, it was not on account of any complaint that Sir George had summoned him:

'As, after a downpour of rain and hail, the clouds break and a ray of sunlight appears in the menacing sky, so did the smile of Sir George when he received me and invited me to sit down.'*

After asking him about his experiences in the hotel and restaurant world

* F. Ferraro, *From Candlelight to Flashlight*.

and about his paintings, he announced to an astonished Ferraro that the directors had decided to appoint him manager of the Berkeley Restaurant.

This restaurant was not well known at the time and on average it was rarely more than half full. Of course he was helped initially by the fact that he had had a very loyal following at the Savoy and a number of his favourite customers now followed him to the Berkeley. On this foundation, he started to build.

I was determined to assert my own personality and to devise means of attracting custom, even at the risk of going against tradition and even of losing my situation. It was all or nothing for me and I set my brains and energy to work.

20. The old Berkeley in Piccadilly.

One of the first items to receive the new manager's attention were the menus:

Menus in those days were printed days in advance. I introduced hand-written ones as we had done at the smart places in Paris and Ostend, not only for dinners ordered in advance, but to be produced a few minutes after the order was given and brought to the table as a compliment, to set before the guests, a document for contemplation and anticipation.

So long as I can remember, I have had an antipathy for printed menus and *cartes du jour;* so much so, that unless commanded to show one, I always went to a table with the menu completed in my mind. I like to compose one to suit the personality of the customer and I must give myself the satisfaction of saying that in nine cases out of ten I managed to guess right.

This kind of highly personal service was bound to make customers into loyal *habitués* and to give the Berkeley a famous name – it did not take too long before this happened and, in order to be sure of being able to discuss menus with real enthusiasm, Ferraro himself always refrained from eating until after all his customers had finished. He had the ability to design a dozen lunches and dinners within the space of one hour without repeating the same dish.

Of course Ferraro's task was not made any easier by the fact that he came to the hotel on his own and had to start from scratch to train everyone in his methods. However, he was such a likeable person that the staff were generally very happy to fall in with his wishes, as was the chef, M. Mesivier. Mesivier was a chef of the classic Escoffier school but nevertheless when Ferraro explained to him that fashions in food were changing and that the Berkeley needed to keep pace with these changes, he accepted it without resentment. Between them, Mesivier and Ferraro created a whole range of new dishes and specialities which soon set all the gourmets of London talking; these were some of the most famous of them:

Prawns Mary Rose
Crab Cappucino
Huîtres Madras
Sole en Papillote

Soufflé de Volaille Dorothy
Lasagnette de Veau au Pignoli
Rissoles d'oeuf Vésuve
Fraises Mimosa
Crêpes Adelina

To whet his customers' appetites Ferraro also created some new cocktails, of which the most famous was his 'Classic Cocktail'. There is not space here to go into detail about all these dishes and specialities but I would like to reproduce here Ferraro's own description of how he first created *Fraises Mimosa*.

It was a quiet sort of evening, and the restaurant looked most beautiful in the twilight, but there were too few diners and too many waiters doing nothing, and I determined to occupy a few of them. So I started to call, first for a trolley, then for two silver basins with ice, which I placed in crystal bowls: then I sent a commis to fetch a box of strawberries, and another several bottles of liqueurs, caster sugar, vanilla, cinnamon, and cold raspberry sauce, after which I started to mix my ingredients before the open window, with the curtains fluttering in the gentle breeze. I rolled the strawberries in the sugar, sprinkled them with port, rolled them in sugar again and put them aside to set. Then, with whipped cream I mixed Benedictine and Curaçao, and added grapefruit juice, blending this detail with raspberry sauce, bringing the mixture to a deep magenta colour. This I poured over the strawberries, and decorated the top with slices of orange and circles of raspberry sauce, dusting the whole lightly with powdered cinnamon – I called it Fraises Mimosa, a name which has the euphonious beauty of a poem. Hardly had I put the new-born sweet into bowls when a party of six came to the door and asked for a table. The head-waiter was taking the order, when the host said, 'The rest of the dinner doesn't matter, but we must have those strawberries that we saw being prepared from our window in the Ritz'. It was an American party, and thereafter there was a steady performance of Fraises Mimosa making before the open window to attract guests of the Ritz to the Berkeley Restaurant.

The result of all Ferraro's innovations and efforts was that in 1925, barely three years after he had been appointed manager, the Berkeley Restaurant which for so long had been scarcely half full had to be enlarged because, every night, customers who had not booked well in advance were being made to sit in the restaurant foyer. But Ferraro did not rest on his laurels at this point – far from it; he became more active than ever and began to cultivate the young. As everyone who has read his P. G. Wodehouse knows, the Berkeley Restaurant was *the* place for young men-about-town and their girlfriends. Bertie Wooster was always tottering in to toy with some sole and a *soufflé chez Ferraro* and this was achieved as a result of several clever policies.

Firstly, Ferraro saw to it that there was a first-rate dance band and for some time the restaurant had the American Frank Harbin Band whose saxophonist, Howard Jacobs, was very well known and, secondly, he attracted supper crowds by seeing to it that some especially good cabaret acts were put on. Beyond this it was his sheer goodness which led to a generation being brought up to regard the Berkeley as *the* place. Let me explain: being such a warm-hearted and delightful person, Ferraro had perhaps a rather closer relationship with his customers than most restaurant managers and so, when anxious mothers organized lunches and dinners for their offspring, they felt (and rightly so) that Ferraro would take a paternal interest and smooth over any difficulty that might arise. Thus, a whole generation began its entertaining at the Berkeley and formed a habit for life. Ferraro also claims that there was one particular table at which couples became engaged by the score and so, if he thought there was a possibility that the man was nearly ready to pop the question, as long as he approved of the match he always gave the romantic couple that particular table.

Ferraro was always immensely considerate to the young and sometimes personally subsidized the dinner of his favourite impoverished clients. Very often young customers would find a bill for two set dinners when they had, in fact, ordered expensive *à la carte* dishes and Ferraro paid the difference. He also helped in other ways – a young but poor peer was arranging a dinner *à deux* for the love of his life and Ferraro recommended a very cheap wine.

'I suggest an Empire still hock from South Africa. It is delicious, with a fine bouquet, and pleasing to the ladies. The bottle is attractive and the price practically nothing.'

'But, Ferraro,' queried the young peer, 'if it's a good wine why so cheap?'

'My lord, it is an Empire product – from South Africa – and even if the wine were a kind of Balsamo (Elixir of Youth) the two words, Empire Product, would prevent the snobs from offering it to their friends.' Naturally Ferraro arranged that the bottle should be wrapped in a napkin so that the lady should not see the label.

As with all good *restaurateurs* and restaurant managers, attention to detail is of the utmost importance and one detail which Ferraro was very keen on was the restaurant's temperature in summer. The Berkeley was, in fact, the first hotel in England to be fully air-conditioned but until this was installed in the 1930s, Ferraro used a large leather-covered tray surrounded with huge blocks of ice with a powerful electric fan in the middle. The ice was decorated with leaves and flowers and when the air-conditioning superseded this, many customers sadly missed it. Ferraro was also very keen on seeing that the food in the restaurant suited the prevailing weather; in the summer, trolleys covered in crushed ice groaned with every kind of sea-food and sea-food cocktail and similar trolleys were loaded up with fresh fruit salad, *fraises Mimosa*, *pêches Melba* and *profiteroles au Chocolat*. In the winter the lighting was increased and warm-coloured bulbs were used with curtains and upholstery of a bright colour to attract the eyes of customers coming in from the cold. Then there would be a display of hot *hors-d'œuvres* warming *plats du jour* such as curries and Irish stews 'so that customers could, without waiting, enjoy a meal and forget all about the depressing weather outside, bathed in a welcome of warmth and happiness'.

For seventeen years the Berkeley Restaurant continued to flourish under Ferraro, its clientele growing both larger and more devoted, and it came as a great blow to many of his loyal followers when he moved on to the Mayfair Hotel in 1939. Nevertheless, his methods and traditions had been so firmly established over the years that the restaurant has never looked back and has never ceased to be one of the most popular hotel restaurants in London, in spite of moving to a completely new site in 1971.

*   *   *

Marcel Boulestin's success in drawing many of the most important members of London Society away from the great traditional restaurants naturally served as an inspiration to others, and one of the first to follow his example was a certain Sovrani, who had risen to a considerable height in the Savoy hierarchy but now yearned to be his own boss. Sovrani acquired a place in Bury Street, St. James', and took with him from the Savoy, as his manager, someone who had already worked under him: John Quaglino. Sovrani's restaurant was a great success and he quickly established a reputation for himself – after all, he had known personally a large number of the Savoy's most distinguished customers. But then he made a rather serious mistake, Italians are always said to be good lovers and Sovrani could not resist having an affair with his manager's attractive wife. Apart from being re-nowned as good lovers, the Italians are also famed for their love of vengeance and John Quaglino was no exception among his fellow-countrymen. However, being a highly civilized man he decided to have his revenge in an honourable and completely non-violent way. He determined to set up a rival restaurant that would be so successful that Sovrani would lose all his customers and have to close down. Obviously, to have the most dramatic effect his restaurant had to be situated as close as possible to Sovrani's and he therefore approached the management of the St. James' Palace Hotel (now the Hotel Meurice), which was just opposite, and asked if he could take over their restaurant and run it under his own name. The St. James' management, which had not been doing particularly well out of its restaurant, liked the idea and so Quaglino's Restaurant was born in 1928 with John as manager and his brother Ernest as head waiter.

21. An impression of Quaglino's from *The Bystander*, June 1932.

Quaglino's was an immediate success and there was no difficulty in filling the restaurant. As manager of Sovrani's John Quaglino had come to know a great many of the regular customers and, just as Sovrani had brought many of his Savoy customers to his restaurant, so now John brought them across the road to Quaglino's. But one of the ironic features of the story was this: over the years Sovrani had become rather a vain and over-confident man and in the early days made a point of telling his customers about his former manager's new place across the street, thinking that they would go, have a good laugh and come back to tell Sovrani how much better his restaurant was than Quaglino's. But this did not happen and the superb food, splendid cabaret and attentive service at Quaglino's won the day. In a year or two Sovrani found his clientele so seriously reduced that he had to close down.

Quaglino's became one of the very greatest restaurants of the 1930s and no female visitor could fail to be impressed by·the gracious way in which John would present her with a flower, as if she was the only person ever to have been favoured in this way. The restaurant was also greatly helped by being adopted as a favourite by the Prince of Wales. His regular presence there secured in an odd sort of way an amnesty that enabled all the diners to come and go without fear of being mentioned in some gossip column the next day; especially if they were dining with someone other than their wife. The Prince (later Edward VIII) was not fond of dressing for dinner and that was absolutely necessary at Quaglino's. John therefore created a special private room for him which exists to this day. There he could come and go and eat with his friends without being seen by other customers.

The Quaglino brothers further extended their influence in the London restaurant world in 1930 by acquiring Le Grand Vatel in Jermyn Street. They reopened it as L'Aperitif Grill which also quickly became a great success. The restaurant moved from there to Brown's Hotel in 1972.

After Quaglino's opened there was a gap of a few years before any other famous restaurant appeared in London. The Great Depression of the early 1930s hit hotels and restaurants very hard and many establishments found their customers ordering more lager than wine and also generally sticking to the cheaper items on the menus. Hotels were particularly hard hit as the tourist trade declined and there were virtually no society balls held while the Depression lasted. The Depression's effects continued into the mid-1930s but at least one *restaurateur* was optimistic enough to believe in a brighter future: that was Mme Prunier.

Paris had been suffering from serious political unrest in the early 1930s and they were worrying times for all who lived there. Accordingly, when Mme Prunier received a letter from an Englishman in January 1934 asking her to open a London branch of Prunier's, she took the suggestion very seriously. There were already signs that the end of the Depression in England might not be far off and so the greater security of having business interests in London as well as Paris was extremely tempting. She was also encouraged by a number of her customers in Paris who told her that, with the possible exception of Scott's, there was no restaurant like Prunier's in the whole of London.

By September 1934 Mme Prunier had acquired the site for her restaurant in St. James' Street and in October she moved to London to prepare for the opening which was scheduled for January 1935. The newspapers announced 'Today Madame Prunier, the Oyster Queen, arrives'.

The restaurant was launched with a great reception on 17 January 1935 at which oysters, caviare, and a variety of other sea-foods were served with kirsch and chocolate mousse to follow. Champagne and a variety of other French white wines were offered and the whole event was a tremendous success. Only Rosa Lewis of the Cavendish was sceptical – she wagered ten guineas that Prunier's would close within six months but she was proved wrong. The restaurant, which was large enough to serve 300 customers, was faced with 600 on the very day after the reception and this pressure was consistently maintained until the outbreak of war in 1939.

In months containing a letter 'r', the menu offered a choice of no less than ten different varieties of oyster but of course there were a great many other items besides. This menu of a special lunch, served a few months after the opening, will give some idea of the range of dishes available:

Les fruits de Mer
Crabes diables
Filets de sole Emile Prunier
Le bar farci et accommodé à la manière Angevine
Faisans rôtis flanqués de cailles aux marrons
Salade de saison
Fromages
Les pêches Melba telles que le mâitre A Escoffier les créa
Une corbeille garnie de friandises

*   *   *

Quentin Crewe, the *bon viveur* and food writer, claims that a greater variety of national cooking is available in London today than in any other capital city in the world and the origins of what one might call this cosmopolitan tradition may be found in the inter-war years. The twenties and thirties saw established a large number of the cheaper continental-style restaurants, many of which were to be found in the Soho area. Of course, some such places had existed even before the turn of the century but their development in the inter-war period was noticeable. Let us now take a look at some leading representatives of each country's cuisine to be found in London in this period.

One of the favourite haunts for those in search of good *bourgeois* French cooking at moderate prices was, L'Escargot Bienvenu in Greek Street which was particularly renowned for its snails and frogs' legs. The *crêpe de volaille* and *carbonade Flamande* were also highly spoken of and the cellar, particularly the red burgundy section, was remarkable for a restaurant in this category. Here two people could eat and drink extremely well for barely 75p.

Some mouth-watering specialities were also to be found at Chez Victor in Wardour Street where a close look at the clientele revealed that many of the tables were occupied by chefs enjoying an evening off from their own restaurants! This in itself is a testament to the excellence of the *coquilles au gratin*, the *cerises à l'eau de vie* and other specialities that were offered. In the summer a truly French atmosphere could be enjoyed by patrons of Antoine in Charlotte Street where one could sit at little tables on the pavement in the shade of four potted bay trees. The set lunches at the equivalent of 10p or $12\frac{1}{2}$p and dinners at 15p or $17\frac{1}{2}$p were astonishing value and though the food was predominantly French, the presence of an Italian as well as a French chef ensured that the *Fritto Misto*, when offered, was excellent. Another French restaurant which was very highly thought of was the Petit Coin de France in Carnaby Street where the *patron* was a philanthropic old gentleman called Père Ober. He was always much in evidence in his tall chef's hat, supervising the cooking and being friendly to his customers. His specialities included *Fricandeau de Veau farci au Jambon*, *pâté truffé maison*, *rillettes de Tours*, and *Marrons au sirop vanille*. I would also mention the Moulin d'Or in Church Street but its gradual adoption by American tourists diluted its true French atmosphere, though the cooking was undoubtedly authentic – tripe and onions being about the only non-French speciality.

Italian restaurants were of course to be found in great numbers but I shall come back to them later, after we have looked at some of the more exotic alternatives.

Those who were in search of something quite out of the ordinary would have been most likely to find it at Tokiwa, a Japanese restaurant in Denmark Street off Charing Cross Road. Unfortunately the menu here was not entirely helpful – a dish called *Mushi-Zushi* was translated as 'Hot Gomoku-Zuchi'. However those who wanted to play safe could go for the *Sukiyaki* which patrons were encouraged to cook to their own taste on a spirit lamp at the table. Green tea was the normal drink to take with a meal here or

Saké. Anyone who wanted to eat in the Japanese manner could squat on the floor beside a low table in the upstairs room.

Chinese restaurants grew in popularity and in number during the inter-war years and, while the Cathay continued to flourish in Piccadilly, a number of worthy rivals sprang up in the surrounding area, one of the best of which was 'The Chinese Restaurant' in Glasshouse Street. Here a total of 211 dishes were offered but I will not go into detail about them as a great many were similar to those offered in the better Chinese restaurants today. However, for the true enthusiast special classic Chinese dishes could be obtained at half a day's notice, provided that a deposit was paid at the time of ordering. These dishes included *Hoong Shiu Yu Chee* (stewed shark's fin Mandarin style), stewed bird's nest with minced chicken and water-lily nut and preserved eggs. Although the clientele of the Chinese Restaurant included many young people who were chiefly attracted by the reasonable prices (a set lunch could be had for 13½p), one reviewer of the restaurant noted that there were usually a number of seasoned Oriental gourmets present, so the cooking must have been of a high standard.

Those American tourists who were beginning to pine for 'cooking like we get back home' and who had either exhausted the American specialities offered by the Savoy or been unable to afford them, could go (as did many English people who could not afford to go to America) to Mrs. Cook's American Restaurant in Denham Street. This was a very simple and cosy place with basket-work chairs and a sanded floor and the specialities included corn on the cob, Chicken Maryland and waffles. Twenty-four varieties of omelettes were offered but probably the best buy was the Kentucky dinner at 27½p which included corn soup, chicken with fried bananas and strawberry shortcake. The coffee was, as one would expect, exceptionally good and, although Mrs. Cook had no licence, wine and beer could easily be sent for.

Although far fewer Russian *émigrés* fled to London after the Revolution than to Paris, there were a number of Russian restaurants to be found in London during the twenties and thirties. At Troika in Denman Street, off Piccadilly, *Bortsch* and Red Caviar Omelettes could be eaten in a room surrounded with paintings of Russia. The *shashlik* and *Bœuf Stroganoff* were also excellent but for more atmosphere many people preferred to go to Chata in Baker Street. Here the friendly charm of the musician-patron M. Szladkowski and the excellent cooking of M. Topolskoff had sufficient magnetic attraction to draw in a very distinguished clientele, indeed Schnabel, the great pianist, was one of the *habitués* whenever he was in

London. The restaurant was furnished in Russian peasant style and M. Szadkowski had such a loyal following that his piace had an almost club-like atmosphere. Like Troika, this restaurant offered *Bortsch* and *Stroganoff*, though there was usually a choice of three different kinds of *Bortsch* and also *Bitki Po Kieffski* – Russian mince cutlets. One of the favourite puddings here was *Nalesniki* – pancakes with cheese and sultanas.

Spanish restaurants also became popular during the inter-war years and probably the best one was Martinez in Swallow Street which is, of course, still flourishing. Great efforts had been made to create a genuine Spanish atmosphere in the restaurant – the green and white décor, the barred windows and the little barrels of sherry all indicated that one had crossed the Pyrenees on entering Martinez. Inevitably the great speciality was *Paella a la Valenciana* and it was first class. *Bon Viveur* noted that particular care was taken with the rice itself so that it was neither too oily nor too dry and it was mixed with liberal portions of chicken pieces, mussels, chillis, and many other ingredients. *Chile con carne* was another great favourite and to end with there was a toothsome dish called *Dolce de Membrillo* – a form of quince cheese.

Some time after Martinez was founded, the *maître d'hôtel*, Señor Bonafont, broke away and founded Majorca in Brewer Street. Here, the walls were adorned with scenes of Majorcan life and the speciality was *Arroz à la Marinera*: 'a harmonious blend of lobster, mussels, and other fish'. Señor Bonafont was also proud of his sweet trolley on which one of the famed dishes was *Orange en Almibar* – oranges candied with their skin. The cellar at the Majorca was an interesting one as it offered quite a wide variety of vintage Spanish wines such as *Marques de Murietta* as well as the more modest *Valdepeñas*. Those who loved a good *Gazpacho* could enjoy it together with a glass of the white house-wine at Barcelona in Beak Street and it could be followed by *Tomales à la Mejicana* – mince and potato wrapped up in maize leaves and served in a hot spicy sauce.

The almost hysterical anti-German atmosphere of the First World War, which was violent enough to force that most English of institutions, the Coburg, to change its name to Connaught, naturally caused German food to go right out of fashion – indeed, at one time, anyone found drinking a glass of hock was liable to be called a traitor. However, as passions cooled down after the war, so German restaurants began to appear again and some of them were very good. Kempinski's in Regent Street offered all the usual dishes: boiled beef, *Holsteiner Schnitzel*, and smoked loin of pork with *Sauerkraut* and mashed potatoes as well as some more exotic masterpieces.

For a first course, for instance, there was an excellent crayfish cocktail in which raw crayfish was served together with a sauce made of onion, cream, lemon, chopped parsley, tabasco, and pepper. Sweetbreads were offered with potato balls and cauliflower on artichoke hearts adorned with *Hollandaise*. Partridge could be ordered garnished with pineapple and a cream sauce and, in the best German tradition, the cakes and pastries were really first class. Kempinski's offered a splendid choice of wines, with particular emphasis on Hocks, Moselles and Sekt.

One German restaurant which had been famous before the First World War and was able to reopen after it was all over was Schmidt's in Charlotte Street. It was also famous for the delicatessen which was attached to it and sold an astonishing variety of smoked meats. Schmidt's was less grand than Kempinski's but nevertheless offered some really good, wholesome German, Austrian, and Hungarian dishes. These included knuckle of pork with cabbage (*Eisbein von Schwein*), *Wiener Schnitzel*, and *Apfelstrudel*, and most of these cost less than 10p.

A successful attempt was made to introduce Danish food to London by the Viking Bar in Berkeley Square. Here a good *smorrebrod* was offered and patrons were invited to drink *aquavit* with their meal. If they found this too formidable an accompaniment to their food they could opt for vintage champagne, which sold for 15p per glass, or Hock, Graves or *vin rosé* which sold at 5p per glass. A number of agreeable Danish dishes were served as alternatives to the *smorrebrod* and these included smoked eel with scrambled eggs, fried force-meat cakes with cucumber salad, bacon and egg cake and *Pyt i Panna* with fried egg (*Pyt i Panna* is a dish consisting of meat, potatoes, and onions fried up together and served with gravy). Nor was Denmark the only Scandinavian country represented in London's gastronomic scene – good Swedish cooking could be readily enjoyed at a restaurant called the Ellikan off Baker Street. Here the *patronne* was Mrs. Ellen Kreuger – a member of the great match-manufacturing family and she was renowned for the freshness and high quality of everything she used in her restaurant. Here, diners were encouraged to begin their meal with the *Smögasbord* – an *hors-d'œuvre* quite similar to the Danish *smorrebrod* with a few additional specialities.

As a main course Mrs. Kreuger recommended her *Slottstek* – braised steak or veal *à la Suedoise* (that is in a rich gravy with onions) or meat balls with brown beans. Lemon cream was a favourite pudding there but I cannot believe that it was particularly representative of Swedish cooking. The Ellikan certainly offered good value, as its set lunches began at $7\frac{1}{2}$p and the best dinner available could be had for $17\frac{1}{2}$p.

Now that we have looked at some of the rarer national restaurants we must return to more familiar territory and look at some of the Italian restaurants. They were by no means an innovation in Soho; some, such as the Florence in Rupert Street and Pagani's in Great Portland Street had been flourishing since the 19th century and patrons of these establishments continued to make regular visits to them to enjoy *mortadella, fritto misto,* and *pollo Pagani* – the latter being cooked in a casserole with mushrooms and button-onions accompanied by a Madeira sauce.

Another of the oldest established Italian restaurants was Pinoli's in Shaftesbury Avenue. Its date of foundation in 1869 means that it must have been among the very first continental restaurants in this country. It is interesting that Pinoli's avoided the temptation to try and become smart and expensive but stuck to the principle that had made it so successful for so long: that of offering superb value in a consistently packed dining-room. In fact it is astonishing just how many people these Italian proprietors were able to serve without lowering their standards – the Bertorelli brothers served between 700 and 800 customers every day at their restaurant in Charlotte Street, though admittedly they had six rooms in which they could accommodate their customers. Bertorelli's was renowned for its wines, almost all of which were shipped by the proprietors themselves, enabling them to offer both Chianti and French wines at moderate prices. In some ways Bertorelli's was a more adventurous restaurant to visit than some of the others as it had an interesting and decidedly Bohemian clientele.

One feature of the Italian restaurants which I find interesting is the extreme loyalty of the clientele. In smart restaurants today one often finds that there is a rather club-like atmosphere and that relatively new customers are almost deliberately made to feel second-class citizens alongside the *habitués*. The success of the Italian proprietors in Soho was that they made you feel so much at home the very first time you went there that you tended to go again and again. Probably the record for loyalty was held by a lady who dined at the Restaurant d'Italie in Greek Street every night without exception from 1907 to 1937. The Restaurant d'Italie, like many other Italian restaurants at that time, always offered some French dishes, though they were more proud of their native specialities such as *Pollo Cacciatore*. Those seeking exclusively Italian food in a restaurant could always go to simple places like the Ristorante del Commercio in Frith Street which was very popular in arty circles. Painters and writers were regularly to be heard holding forth on their pet subjects over the *Zabaglione* and the delicious *Crêpes à la Dilke* which were served with honey.

But of all the Italian restaurants in Soho, probably the most famous one in the thirties was Leoni's Quo Vadis in Dean Street which had opened with only seven tables in October 1926 and, as a result of Leoni's hard work, gradually expanded into something greater while retaining its personal atmosphere. Leoni was a most dedicated *restaurateur* and in his book *I shall die on the Carpet* he explained the role of the good *patron* as follows:

> He is not there simply to supply food and wine for he must also provide an atmosphere in which the customers will enjoy both and not eat or drink as a dismal penance. Tears will never stimulate the digestive juices as well as laughter does.

It was this genial approach, combined with good cooking and the use of fresh ingredients from the market, that gradually brought him success. Another factor which aroused interest in the restaurant was the art exhibitions put on there by the Grubb Group. These began when an impoverished English artist called Edward Craig became one of Leoni's most regular lunchtime customers. Although Craig usually only paid 8p for lunch, a time came when he could no longer afford even this much. Leoni was kind enough to say that he should continue to come as often as he wished and just sign his bills, which would be paid when he did eventually make some money. Craig was so touched by this that he decided to try and help produce some more regular customers for Leoni. One of the ways in which he was able to do this was by forming an organization called the Grubb Group which put on regular exhibitions at the restaurant. The publicity obtained by this idea, which was completely new to London though well-established in Paris, brought customers flocking to the Quo Vadis, many of whom became regulars. At the same time, as Leoni refused to take any commission on the work sold, Craig was able to help both himself and many of his artist friends to establish themselves and sell their work; most of them would have found an exhibition at a gallery beyond their means.

*   *   *

In this age, where so many of us travel round the country with one or more of the guides to good food in our luggage, it may be a little hard for those of us who have grown up since the war to realize just how uninteresting food was outside London thirty or forty years ago. Harry Yoxall, Chairman of the International Wine and Food Society, was unfortunate enough to be obliged to go out of London on business frequently during the inter-war years and he does not recall his gastronomic experiences at this time with much enthusiasm:

'Outside London, Britain was an absolute desert in the 1920s but in the 1930s it was rather better. It was a penance to eat away from London.' But Mr. Yoxall does admit that there were a few exceptions to the rule and that it was possible to eat very well in some of the hotel restaurants operated by the railway companies as well as at a few independent places such as the Royal Clarence at Exeter, the Angel at Bury St. Edmunds and the Compleat Angler at Marlow.

It was the railway companies who were the real pioneers of gastronomy in the provinces and no doubt it will come as a surprise to some people to learn that the first provincial French restaurant complete with a French chef opened at the Midland Hotel in Manchester in 1904. Indeed, at that time the Midland boasted three national restaurants: American, German, and French. All this was possible only because the hotel manager was a man of outstanding ability. His name was William Towle and he, together with his son Arthur, was almost entirely responsible for creating the high

22. Adelphi Hotel Restaurant, Liverpool.

standards which the British Transport Hotels, the successor of railway companies, maintains to this day.

The next important provincial French restaurant to appear was at the Adelphi Hotel in Liverpool. It opened on the day of the Grand National in 1914. One article in the railway archives describes it as follows:

It is hard to avoid superlatives in describing the new Restaurant. This delightful salon has been carried out in Louis XIV period of decoration and furnishing. Here the most epicurean tastes are met with refinements in cooking, service and wines that vie with those of the finest restaurants in London, Paris or Vienna or indeed in any part of the world.

Unfortunately it has not been possible to find an Adelphi menu of 1914 but the menu of the dinner given to the delegates of the American Hotels Association when they visited the hotel in 1926 will give some idea of what it was capable of producing:

Grapefruit
Caviar Frais
Tortue claire au vieux Madère
Saumon d'Ecosse Epicurienne
Selle d'Agneau de lait Mireille
Petits Pois frais à l'Anglaise
Pommes nouvelles Parisiennes
Poussins sous la cendre
Salade Orientale
Asperges vertes, Sauce Divine
Soufflé Glacé Caprice
Panier de Friandises
Corbeille de Fruits
Moka

The Adelphi was in fact one of the most famous hotels in Britain during the inter-war years. It was visited by members of the Royal Family on numerous occasions as well as by foreign princes and was regularly used by American ambassadors.

Numerous other fine restaurants were opened by the railway companies in the years following the First World War including the three most important Scottish ones which we shall come to in the chapter on Scotland, and the Queen's Hotel in Leeds whose Harewood Restaurant, which opened in 1934, was of an exceptionally high standard for the time. But the two provincial restaurants that will probably live on longest in people's memories were independent ones: the Hind's Head at Bray and the Spread Eagle at Thame. These were the first two restaurants to establish such a national reputation among the *cognoscenti* that they attracted people to make special journeys to visit them. Never before could the *Michelin Guide*'s expression *mérite un détour* have been applied to any British establishment. Let us start with the Spread Eagle for no better reason than that I live only a little over two miles away from it!

23. The Hind's Head, Bray.

After a lengthy history as a favourite farmers' pub (there were then twenty-eight pubs in Thame for the benefit of the 3,500 inhabitants) the Spread Eagle was acquired in 1922 by John Fothergill who must have come as something of a shock to the farmers and they to him. When I say 'favourite pub', it was deserted for most of the time except on Tuesdays – market day – when more than a hundred farmers would invade it simultaneously. At first Fothergill, though he did not like the farmers and probably made little effort to get on with them, attempted to run it on more or less traditional lines. Once, in the hope of boosting the week-end trade slightly, he put up a notice in the bar saying:

24. The Spread Eagle, Thame.

'Wanted – thirty good men to eat the following dinner on Saturday January 20th (1923).' The menu offered for 20p was:

Tomato Soup
Fish – brown stew
Venison
Jugged Hare
Plum Pudding
Toasted Cheese
Filberts

Twenty-five people agreed to come, but as only thirteen turned up and very few drinks were ordered, Fothergill made no profit and decided not to bother with this sort of venture again. Instead, he almost deliberately began to discourage most of the people who made up his clientele. He disciplined the farmers on market day in a way they were not used to and gradually put their backs up. He put off many of his would-be commercial traveller guests in various ways and even brought to an end the regular Freemasons' dinners at the Spread Eagle, which his predecessor had strongly recommended him to serve at cost price by way of advertisement. One commercial traveller particularly asked for a steak. Fothergill said he had none and that, in any case, it would have been very tough but recommended his lamb. The traveller exclaimed that he had eaten steak five days a week for thirty years and did not intend to do otherwise now. Fothergill accordingly went to the butcher and ordered the toughest piece of meat from the most recently killed carcass in the shop. The traveller never returned. Gradually a new kind of clientele began to replace the old one. Fothergill's many friends in society passed the word round and people became curious enough to drive down from London. Word also reached

25. John Fothergill.

Oxford and a steady flow of *bon viveur* dons and rich undergraduates began to appear, though Fothergill never approved of the latter – indeed his disapproval of this sector of society led to his making a rather unfortunate mistake when, one day, he received a letter from the Queen's College, Oxford, asking him to prepare a special dinner for two, each course being minutely specified. Fothergill assumed the letter had come from a rich young undergraduate and, being always keen to teach people a lesson, he 'winkled their oysters', substituted chicken for pheasant and stuffed cucumbers for aubergine. When the diners arrived they turned out to be T. W. Allen, Fellow of the Queen's College, and Dr. Cowley, Curator of the Bodleian – two of the most outstanding gourmets in the entire university. At least he was able to serve them with good wine – a Lafite of 1907 and an Yquem of 1914.

Robin McDouall, who knew Fothergill well, recalled a number of specialities of the Spread Eagle in an article for the *Daily Telegraph Magazine*. These included *Gjetost* – Scandinavian cheese cut paper thin and served on home-made water biscuits, and black soup made of brown beans and laced with brown sherry.

> I think the next course was usually some excellent roast chicken or roast meat with some exotic vegetables – cabbage coloured with beetroot or beetroot coloured with cabbage. Then came the puddings, of which our favourites were Thame Tart and Mavrodaphne Trifle (Mavrodaphne is a sort of Greek version of Marsala).

The Thame Tart, Mr. McDouall informs us, was made of pastry, raspberry jam, lemon curd, and cream in layers. The clientele of the Spread Eagle was really quite extraordinary, as in addition to the various categories I have mentioned, one could easily bump into H. G. Wells, André Simon, Arnold Dolmetsch or G. K. Chesterton. Evelyn Waugh described Fothergill as 'Oxford's only civilizing influence'.

Fothergill did not stint in his effort to furnish his distinguished customers with the finest ingredients. As he says in his *Innkeeper's Diary**:

> When I took this shop, I thought round for all the things I had found best wherever I'd been and sent for them. So Kate [his wife] pays regular bills for food-stuff in Athens, France, Norway, Jaffa, and Italy. And of English things we have daily from three bakers three different kinds of bread made from flours that I have forced upon them, besides the breads we make ourselves, cheese from East Harptree, salt from Malden,

* *An Innkeeper's Diary* (Chatto and Windus, 1931).

mustard from Leighton Buzzard, sausages – after a search all over England – from Glenthorn in Thame, books from the Book Society, bacon, found by accident, from the International Stores . . . surely this is better than buying all your stuff from an 'Hotel Purveyor' . . . surely this is better and more difficult than having one *specialité gastronomique*?

Fothergill sold the Spread Eagle in 1931 having lost, if we can trust his diary, a considerable sum over the years, and went to the Royal Hotel at Ascot. The Spread Eagle was never quite the same again, but it lives on to this day and thrives under his successors.

The other great *restaurateur* of the inter-war period outside London was Barry Neame and he too took a firm line with clients who did not please him.

Neame first rose to distinction in a field only remotely connected with gastronomy, for when the Savoy Hotel opened its own laundry a few years after the end of the First World War, Barry Neame was its first manager.

26. Barry Neame.

Rumour has it (though I have not been able to prove this) that the laundry arranged a works outing to Bray-on-Thames one day and it was on this outing that Neame first came across the Hind's Head. The rumour goes on to say that it was at this moment that he first resolved to become the proprietor of the Hind's Head and to make it a famous establishment, though this did not happen for a while. Instead, he left the Savoy laundry in December 1923, taking the manageress with him, and together they opened a rival establishment called the Bluebird Laundry only a short distance away.

History does not appear to record whether or not the Bluebird Laundry in Clapham was a huge success under Neame but it does record that the Hind's Head was, and this success was based primarily on his cellar and his personality. The food was generally of a high standard, but simple: beef and treacle tart with game in season. He also went in for giblet soup, which he liked to serve with a José Ramirez Solera of 1858.

Maurice Healy, writing of Neame in his book *Stay me with Flagons,** had this to say:

> My dear friend, Barry Neame, who has shown that the best cellars need not be found in large places, has a claret list that boasts over one hundred Chateau-bottled wines. At his hospitable table one may sit down to compare half a dozen vintages of the same wine or the same vintage in half a dozen wines.

Healy recalls that, on one occasion, Neame produced a bottle of Yquem 1869 and that when this turned out to be a little disappointing, replaced it with a bottle of Yquem 1921 (a wine which many experts consider to be the greatest Sauternes of all time).

Although Barry Neame was a big, florid, genial-looking man and apparently the ideal type of 'mine Host', he could, as I have said, be very unkind to customers who chose their wines badly or ordered cheap wines, and at least one former customer recalls that he had a slightly distressing way of assuming that everyone he did not know personally was totally ignorant of matters gastronomic. Nevertheless, he attracted a remarkable circle of *bon viveurs* such as André Simon, Maurice Healy, Vyvyan Holland, and Ian Campbell, as well as a number of the leading lights of theatreland.

Even during the war, Neame was able, when he really wanted to, to work wonders. In October 1944 Neame asked Simon if he would like him to put on a meal for 100 members of the Wine and Food Society in two batches of fifty. Simon was absolutely delighted with the suggestion and the feast consisted of piping-hot vegetable soup, pheasants 'that were exactly right: tender, moist, tasty, hung just long enough, not high, quite perfect, and as much as you cared for'. This was followed by the famous treacle tart.

The wines were, in spite of the war, fully up to Neame's high standards. On both days a Bâtard Montrachet of 1929 was served first, followed by Château Lascombes of the same year from an Imperial.

It was sad that Neame gave up the Hind's Head not long after this lunch and, although he did acquire another inn in Hampshire, it was never quite the same thing.

Meanwhile, the restaurants in London, which had gradually recovered from the Great Depression, were hit by the Munich crisis of 1938. The crisis caused reservations to drop dramatically, which is perhaps only natural

* *Stay me with Flagons* (Michael Joseph, 1940).

when one considers that nothing is worse for the digestion than anxiety. However, the sun shone again when Chamberlain stepped off his Imperial Airways flight holding a little piece of paper signed by Hitler and so the restaurants filled up and, for a few months, tables had to be reserved well in advance. But the war clouds did not roll away for long and finally, in September, the great blow fell; the astonished staff of the Savoy saw Sir George Reeves-Smith walk into the hotel on the morning of 4 September 1939 in a lounge suit and a bowler-hat. It was the first time they had ever seen him wearing something other than a morning coat or white tie. Nothing less than the outbreak of war could have effected such a transformation.

Chapter 4

WAR AND RECOVERY

WE did not learn from our mistake: as regards food supplies, the Second World War found us just as ill-prepared as the First. In the two decades of peace before the Second World War the British agricultural sector shrank, just as it had in the half century before the First World War. In the years of peace between the two world wars, the number of persons employed on farms fell about 30 per cent and the area under the plough was reduced by about 25 per cent. Some seven-eighths of Britain's wheat and flour and over two-thirds of her total calories came from across the seas.

It was, therefore, extremely fortunate that Germany only had a few submarines in action during the first eighteen months of the war, otherwise we should almost certainly have suffered real famine. It is estimated that there was on average only fifteen enemy submarines on duty in the Atlantic during this period and yet, because of the paucity and inadequacy of our defensive measures at that time, even these were in a position to inflict very severe damage. The German submarine activity reached its zenith early in 1943 but luckily by this time the Allies were much better equipped to deal with the problem.

At least the Government did manage to some extent, after the war had started, to make up for lost time with agricultural policies which were both intelligent and efficient. Farmers could only keep cattle if they produced enough foodstuffs to feed them and have a surplus on top of that, thus the Government ensured that each acre of land produced the greatest calorific value in food. Naturally this meant a severe shortage of meat; the number of pigs in Britain fell by 50 per cent during the war and chicken and cattle fell very considerably in numbers, but it did also mean that imports of animal foodstuffs could be reduced by 55 per cent and at times by even as much as 75 per cent.

In spite of all these restrictions, the average Briton's diet during the war was actually better than it had been before – as had been true in the First World War – and, because the overall quantity of food was so closely rationed, restaurants became extremely popular as a way of saving coupons. Also, more people than ever before were in a position to eat in restaurants during the war because of the price restrictions that were imposed on them.

Having thus taken a preliminary look at the food supply situation, let us now take a closer look at how the restaurant world coped with all its problems.

The very first problem that restaurants faced was, fortunately, short-lived and lasted only for the duration of the period known as the 'phoney war', that is the period before air-raids began.

The problem was that customers suddenly disappeared. Everyone who could leave London immediately did so and for more than six months the city was almost empty. Then, just as the blitz was about to begin, people began to drift back and make full use of restaurants again. The most critical problem of all was therefore solved and, as soon as there were customers again, *restaurateurs* began to tackle the other problems of shortages of food and wine supplies, and of staff. To give some idea of the extent of the shut-down during the 'phoney war', the Savoy had to close down the Grill Room altogether and its chef, Virlogeux, went off to the Dorchester. The Savoy Restaurant was also closed because it was not considered safe enough and meals from the restaurant kitchen were served in the heavily reinforced Abraham Lincoln Room. Stanley Jackson in his book on the Savoy paints a depressing picture of the early days of the war:

> Latry set himself the task of maintaining his reputation on an austerity budget that meant no cooking-oil, little sugar or butter and ersatz mayonnaise. . . . The man who was reputed to know two hundred ways of preparing an egg now practised almost as many enigmatic variations on the humble swede.

Restaurants became extremely skilled at improvising and substituting. At Martinez the unspecified though perfectly acceptable *escalope panné* was in fact made out of pigeon and, with a little practice, the chef found he could make such a good Spanish omelette out of powdered egg that many people could not tell the difference. Whale meat was tried out but it did not sell well and was dropped. Before the war, Martinez had an average bill of £1,000 per month for chickens, a figure which fell, after the introduction of rationing, to £35. Its place had to be taken by pigeon, rabbit and guinea-fowl, none of which was rationed.

Prunier's was particularly badly hit by the fish ration which was only 2 lb for every 200 customers. The restaurant therefore usually only bought what might be called 'luxury' fish such as lobster and scallops. Fortunately, the situation was eased by the Government releasing extra quantities of frozen fish at Bank Holidays and other times. One winter Mme Prunier was able to buy very large quantities of cod in this way and serve it simply as 'poisson' with the name of the sauce. Prunier's was able to secure a reasonable supply of chickens but the chef complained that he thought they had been fattened on barbed-wire because they were so tough! Prunier's 'pigeon' *pâté*, which many customers were absolutely delighted with, was in fact made of rooks. Naturally their wartime mayonnaise was made of powdered egg and their 'cream' of soya-bean extract. Their butter ration was so small that it had to be blended with whale oil.

Simpson's in the Strand was very badly affected by the shortages, as its reputation was built on its splendid roast beef and its saddles of mutton, both of which disappeared from the menu at a very early stage in the war. Hugh Wontner, Chairman of the Savoy Group, was able to help Simpson's a little by arranging with Cameron of Lochiel to supply venison from Scotland. He also paid visits to Aberdeen to buy herrings for smoking and these were a popular feature at Simpson's during these years.

At the Savoy, after Latry's retirement in 1941, Dutrey became chef and began to experiment with all sorts of new and strange ingredients. Stanley Jackson says that on one occasion someone suggested to Dutrey that he should use owls as a supplement to the rations:

'What do I do with an owl?' he asked.

'Stuff it?' suggested a sous-chef innocently.

To make sure that restaurant customers could not be too greedy, the Government brought in a number of restrictions in the spring of 1942, the most important of which decreed that the maximum charge for food was to be 25p. To help the more luxurious establishments it was agreed that a 'house charge' of up to 32½p could also be made. At Prunier's this charge was 27½p for lunch and 32½p for dinner but this was reduced in October 1942 to 12½p and 20p. At Martinez it was a more humble 5p at lunch and 7½p at dinner. It was also decreed that meals should be restricted to three courses or only two courses if bread was served.

Generally speaking, restaurants were good about keeping to the rules though there was one restaurant which was often patronized by a leading Spanish journalist and where the rules were sometimes bent a little. This journalist was in the habit of regularly ordering more than the specified number of courses and so one day he asked a waiter why the management had put up a notice saying 'We request our clients to co-operate with the waiters and see that the rules are observed'. The reply was, 'That's only there for the English'.

Inevitably there was a large and flourishing black market but it probably only served the rather less significant restaurants; for very well-established places the risk was too high and in any case most good managements would

27. M. Bonvin of Kettner's.

genuinely not have wanted to do anything so unpatriotic as supporting the black market. It was because the Savoy was so good about playing by the rules that Vic Oliver said one night, when he was appearing in a cabaret at the Savoy's shelter. 'We are employing very small waiters tonight to make the sandwiches look bigger'. One of the few well-known restaurants to get into trouble over using the black market was Kettner's and, as a result, it was closed down in 1942. Happily it was acquired after a few months by the Monnickendam family who brought in M. Bonvin as manager. He had been head waiter at the Ecu de France until that time. M. Bonvin was thus faced with the monumental task of restarting the restaurant in the middle of the war, but he accomplished this most successfully. The first problem was to obtain food and wine supplies; everything had been sold off at the time of the closure and there were no tinned, dried or otherwise preserved foods in stock. He was fortunate enough to be on friendly terms with a man who owned a loch in Scotland who was able to send Kettner's regular supplies of salmon-trout, as well as hares and poultry. M. Bonvin also found he could obtain supplies of kid, which was not rationed, and so they used this as their basic meat and cooked it in a great many different ways. Only their most regular customers became really tired of it. For first courses the choice was very limited: usually there was an *hors-d'œuvres* made almost exclusively of various types of salad and sometimes there was an egg dish, made, of course, from powdered eggs. For desert there was ice-cream and stewed fruit sweetened with saccharine and rarely anything else.

Cheese was particularly hard to come by in restaurants during the war and most places therefore held such supplies as they were able to obtain in reserve for their best customers. One waiter told me that customers would sometimes give a surprised sniff when he passed their table. The explanation, he said, was not that he had failed to wash but that he had hidden away a piece of rather strong cheese in his tail-coat pocket for a favourite customer.

The 25p limit and the house charges left the more luxurious restaurants very badly off and they found that the only way to compensate for their losses was to make a heavy charge for wines. Naturally they put the price of spirits up but these were available in such small quantities anyway that they could not make a significant contribution. Most restaurants were lucky if they could obtain as much as two bottles of whisky and gin per day, and when this was sold nothing more was available until the next day. Wines were also scarce but they were not rationed and supplies did continue to come in in small quantities throughout the war. Some idea of the inflated wine prices of the war years may be obtained by comparing the prices of Claridge's 1938 list with those of the Berkeley for 1942.

From Claridge's Wine List 1938:

Champagne

Ayala Extra Dry 1926	60p
Veuve Clicquot Dry England	67½p
Bollinger Special Cuvée very dry N.V.	55p

Red Bordeaux

St. Julien Supérieur 1917	25p
Chat. Mouton Rothschild 1925	70p
Chat. Margaux 1923	90p

Red Burgundy

Beaune 1916	30p
Chambertin 1923	50p
Richebourg 1923	80p

*   *   *

From the Berkeley Wine List 1942:

Champagne

Ayala 1934	£2·87½
Bollinger 1934	£7·50

Red Bordeaux

St. Emilion Supérieur 1922	£2·92½
St. Emilion 1934	£4·12½
Chat. Lafite 1928	£6·12½

Red Burgundy

Beaujolais 1937	£3·25
Beaune Superieur 1934	£4·50
Chambolle Musigny Etampé 1934	£6·00

A glass of sherry at the Berkeley in 1942 could cost anything from 22½p to 30p though this is perhaps more understandable when one reflects that at one auction held in aid of the Red Cross, sherry was being sold at £5 per bottle!

Martinez was fortunate in having a good stock of Spanish brandy when the war broke out but it caused them a little embarrassment: when 'wood alcohol' began to be served in some of the less reputable restaurants, people were warned that they should look out for a 'slightly smoky' taste. Unfortunately Spanish brandy has a slightly smoky taste and this frightened away some of the potential brandy drinkers at Martinez although only the genuine stuff was served there.

Next to supply and financial problems, the most serious difficulty restaurants had to overcome was the shortage of staff. As soon as war was declared all German waiters and managers were swiftly interned, while staff of friendly foreign nationalities often left to join their own forces. Naturally, all young English male staff were called up and a further blow was struck when Italy entered the war as that meant that all Italian staff, except for a few naturalized Italians who had not become members of the Italian Club (which was regarded as a highly dangerous Fascist organization) were interned.

One of the many to suffer this fate was Peppino Leoni, the proprietor of the Quo Vadis, and he was particularly fortunate in avoiding sailing to Canada on the *Andorada Star* – a ship which was attacked and sunk by what was almost certainly an Italian submarine while taking Italian internees to Canada.

Mme Prunier has written vividly about the difficulties caused by staff being called up*:

> The mobilisation hit us hard, three-quarters of the cooks were French and all were called to the colours; my restaurant manager Guyot, and my chef, Cochois, were both in their forties and fathers of families but they too, were ordered to leave at three days' notice. Cochois and his team worked up to midday of the day they were going, so as to leave everything in order. The previous day a new French chef, M. Cadier, had reported for duty. It was only later I learned he had missed the wedding of his son, who was one of those called up, so as not to let the Maison down. M. Cadier had brought some of his team with him, and older cooks had come out of retirement, but all the same, I felt bewildered

* *La Maison* (Longmans, 1957).

and helpless as I said goodbye to Cochois and his men whom I had known for so long and worked with so well.

Naturally, many retired cooks and waiters followed the example of the men at Prunier's and came out of retirement to fill the gaps left by their colleagues who had been called up. But there were also a number of other ways of solving the problem: staff from neutral countries such as Spain and Switzerland did, in many cases, stay on and a great many restaurants found that they could employ English waitresses instead of waiters. The Mayfair Hotel employed Czechs and Jewish refugees from Germany, while Kettner's solved its problem by employing mess-room personnel who had been invalided out of the Navy. This worked well as the men found it very easy to adapt from mess-room waiting to serving in a restaurant and once a nucleus of these men had been formed, they were usually able to call on one of their friends to join the staff whenever an extra person was needed.

28. Mme Prunier.

Other restaurants helped to solve their staff shortage by drawing on the staff fire services. Mr. G. E. Osborne of the Hyde Park Hotel was employed in this way: he had served before the war as a steward on a Cunarder, often spending his longer periods of shore leave working as a waiter. In 1940, after registering with the R.A.F., he heard that anyone over thirty years old could volunteer to work in the police or fire service instead of being called up and he decided to opt for the fire service. His duty periods were two days on followed by one day off and, as the fire service did not pay very well, he decided to continue working as a waiter on his days off. In this capacity he helped to run functions in the Marie Antoinette Room at the Ritz.

Restaurants certainly had a special atmosphere during the war years and on the whole morale, on the part of both staff and customers, was surprisingly high. There were several bomb disasters, the worst of which was a direct hit on the Café de Paris while it was crowded with several hundred people dining and dancing. But in spite of everything, people were absolutely determined to enjoy themselves when they went out to eat and so, no matter how ordinary the food set before them, they were enthusiastic about it and waiters and chefs responded accordingly. Mr. Negri, now manager of the Empress, was particularly struck by the wartime atmosphere:

> People were more friendly than ever before. If anyone knew a joke, they would tell it to everyone in the restaurant and, whereas before the war, people would come into a restaurant without looking at diners sitting at other tables, they now made a point of being friendly to each other. The war brought a pleasant kind of informality.

Guy Deghy and Keith Waterhouse commented on the change of atmosphere in their book *The Café Royal**:

> The war brought fresh colours into the Brasserie; if in 1914 khaki had become its predominant colour, early in the last war a young man wearing a maroon blouse, dark blue trousers, cowhide boots, a white astrakhan hat, and a blue great-coat with many medal ribands and a dagger could be seen having supper with a lady in the Café. He was a Finnish airman.

Dancing continued in most places where it had flourished before the war though not till such a late hour, and live broadcasts were regularly made from such places as the Savoy and Martinez where Edmundo Ross played in the cellar and people danced on an improvised square of linoleum. This also helped to keep people's spirits up and enabled them to escape, at least for the duration of a dinner, from the harsh realities surrounding them.

It was a great achievement on the part of André Simon to keep the Wine and Food Society going through the war years and it did a lot of good. The Society was not able to organize any lunches or dinners between May 1940 and October 1944, but its magazine, *Wine and Food*, continued to come out at regular intervals throughout the war, keeping alive its members' interest in gastronomy and giving them helpful advice as to how to make the most of whatever was available. The menu of the lunch held at the Connaught Rooms in October 1944 was not spectacular, nor was the Algerian wine which was served with it, but the event, which is famous in the Society's history, was an enormous success. This was the menu:

* *The Café Royal* (Hutchinson, 1955).

Scallops
Partridge Bonne Femme
Apple and sultana pudding

'Of course, everybody knew that Partridge was the stage name of some bird that never was a partridge, but anybody's guess. They had wings and legs but no feet, which made Barry Neame say they were seagulls. But I am sure that he was wrong.'*

*   *   *

At last it was all over – the war ended and, as people set out to go to their favourite restaurants in the evening with no fear of bomb attacks, they hoped that there would, before too long, be a return to pre-war standards. Here, however, they were in for an unpleasant shock, for the immediate effect of peace was to make supplies even more scarce and to remove the rather relaxed happy atmosphere that had existed during the war years. Everyone seemed to be in a slightly 'Bolshie' mood just after the war and this was bound to have its effect on the standard of the service in many places. There was no war to give restaurant staff the feeling that they were, in their own way, doing their bit for the country and there was no good food and little wine about to enable them to take a pride in what they served.

In some ways the post-1945 diet was more frugal than the wartime ration. Even supplies of bread were acutely short and for a time it had to be rationed although it had never been rationed during the war. The result of all this was that no improvement at all could be made in British gastronomy until rationing ended and so there was a long period in which some restaurants' standards declined while others, by making a special effort, maintained their wartime level. Many restaurants lost a considerable proportion of their regular customers at this time and the difficulty of winning back their reputation later on was very considerable.

It was not until 1950 that the 25p limit on meal prices was lifted and even then the position was not greatly improved as rationing continued, though less severely, right up until 1954. 1950 is, however, a significant date in the history of British gastronomy because, in addition to the lifting of the price restriction, it was also the year in which a certain historian and *bon viveur* called Raymond Postgate founded the Good Food Club. It was a club with no list of members, no subscriptions and no clubhouse. It was, as he himself said, 'A society of people having a double purpose: to improve

* André Simon, *In the Twilight* (Michael Joseph, 1969).

29. Raymond Postgate.

British cooking and service and to communicate to each other information about places where the cooking, cellar, and courtesy came up to proper standards'.

The communication of information was achieved by members sending reports to Postgate about the places they visited. He then edited the reports and incorporated them into the first *Good Food Guide* which was published in 1951. Much may be learned about the general state of British gastronomy at the time by looking at the preface to that first *Guide* in which Postgate had this to say:

The book does not provide material for a 'gastronomic' tour such as can be arranged in France, because the standard of cooking is not, frankly, sufficiently high to justify that rather portentous claim. But they [the results of the first year's research] are the first mapping of an unexplored country. . . . There is no other way that I can see of bringing the force of public opinion to bear on British catering than through some such guide as this. For fifty years now complaints have been made against British cooking and no improvement has resulted. Indeed, it is quite arguable that worse meals are served today in hotels and restaurants than were in Edwardian days. It is certain that the last great war lowered standards even more and that there has only been a small recovery since. British food, indeed, is sometimes said to be the worst in the world bar American. Yet there is no reason why British cooking should be worse than, say, French . . . it remains worse only because public discontent is unorganized and (it must be admitted) sometimes also ignorant.

The preface also reveals how serious the supply situation remained in 1951:

> Remember, in ordering your food, the particular shortages from which we still suffer. The most serious of these is the shortage of butcher's meat. Unfortunately, roasting and grilling, at which the British used to excel, call specifically for butcher's meat and innkeepers feel obliged to offer roasts and grills when they really have not got the materials. Call for chops, steaks, and roast beefs, therefore, only in the country where they are more plentiful, and in towns where the restaurant quite obviously and satisfactorily makes a speciality of them.

Also in the Preface, Postgate advised diners to make a point of complaining where food was bad and giving special thanks where it was actively good. He encouraged people to try to know what they wanted: 'If the Enemy hears one of you say "I'll have whatever you do, dear", he immediately decides he has not serious foes to encounter.'

Another of his rules was to always ask the waiter 'What is good today?' or if you are in Soho 'What is the *"Specialité" de la Maison?*' 'If he answers the equivalent of "everything is excellent" then he is a bad waiter and it is probably a bad restaurant. But persist; and he will probably refer to a seedy-looking man in a boiled shirt (or a cross woman in black silk). That is the person who knows, and from him or her you will find out the one thing that is eatable.'

Postgate also appeals to girlfriends and wives neither to discourage complaints too much nor to encourage their escorts to make a full-scale scene, but to give them steady and calm support.

It is, of course, absurd to try and pinpoint the exact moment when restaurants really began to return to their pre-war levels of cooking and service, but probably it would be true to say that by 1952 the process was almost complete. Mme Prunier felt that 1952 marked her restaurant's return to normality but as she said, 'We had a long and hard struggle to face before we came back into our own again'.

The 1952 *Good Food Guide* also suggests that this would be about the right date for the return to normality. In its entry of that year for Boulestin it said:

> Between the wars, under the famous Marcel Boulestin, this was probably the best restaurant in London. Like others, it slid down during the war, but it is now coming back to its primaeval glory.

In the previous year, the entry for L'Ecu de France had read:

Before the war this was the finest French Restaurant in London; the chef was decorated with the Legion of Honour. It dipped heavily during the war but it is recovering now.

Of course, almost all the grand old places recovered: the Savoy, Quaglino's, L'Etoile, the Café Royal and others too numerous to mention. But it is not in their recovery that the real interest in the early 1950s lies: it lies in the story of the birth of a new kind of cooking and a new kind of restaurant which was to reach its highest level at places such as Parkes' in the 1960s. There is no accepted name for this sort of cooking – one cannot really call it a school of cooking – so the best I can do is to describe it as 'amusing' and 'original'. Of course, one had always been able to obtain exotic foreign dishes by ordering them in advance at the Savoy and other leading restaurants, but until the early 1950s out of the ordinary food did not exist at modest prices and nor were there informal, small, cosy restaurants.

This new style of restaurant came into existence because a number of food-loving amateurs came into the business in the fifties and broke all the established rules with new combinations and fresh ideas. Inevitably, a large number of these new restaurants failed but several were immensely successful and the reason for their success was that they had no direct rivals. All the other restaurants in London served very much the same sort of food, that is: smoked salmon, steak pie, roast beef and so on and they therefore had very severe competition to face. The way was thus wide open for these enthusiastic amateurs with their unique and interesting specialities.

The new type of cooking, cooking which bent all the accepted rules and gave scope to the chef's imaginative talents, seems to have had its origin in two places: the Ox on the Roof in King's Road, Chelsea, and the little restaurant run by Bill Stoughton at the Watergate Theatre Club in Charing Cross Road. Both opened in 1950 (though the Ox on the Roof had opened earlier as a sort of delicatessen-cum-buffet) and both were highly successful.

Bill Stoughton came to England from Australia and at first tried to pursue a career as an actor but it did not go very well so, instead, he opened a little restaurant at the Watergate Theatre Club. Here it was possible to eat from the time the play ended until about two or three in the morning. Stoughton had had no proper training as a chef but he enjoyed cooking and found that he could reproduce dishes he had enjoyed in France and other places quite well working merely on instinct. As rationing was still in force, the early dishes were really quite simple though at that time they must have seemed very special to his customers. One of the early specialities was tinned kidneys with a wine and mushroom sauce, served with rice, and to the palates of those who had suffered the cooking of the war years and the recovery period such an imaginative creation must have been a joy. As rationing restrictions eased and he discovered more and more amusing dishes through his travels, the food became exciting and the fact that he was patronized by so many theatrical celebrities ensured that glowing reports of his culinary skill quickly spread far and wide.

The proprietors of the Ox on the Roof were called Alfred and Ruby – he was of Slavonic origin and she came from the East End, and both of them had a flair for cooking, inventing dishes and creating in their restaurant a warm *sympathique* atmosphere. The first edition of the *Good Food Guide* described it as 'A gay little restaurant where the owners personally serve you with snails, Virginia-style ham and chocolate gâteau'. Other specialities included spit-roasted chicken, *ratatouille*, *aioli*, *cassoulet*, *tortillas*, and *arroz alla Valenciana*.

It is probably hard for people today who are used to finding all these items on the menus of many of the restaurants they patronize, to understand how astonishing it was to find them in the London of the early 1950s. To say Alfred and Ruby were pioneers is an understatement – the truth is they were so far ahead of their time that they should be regarded as the fore-runners of the pioneers.

30. Dr. Hilary James

Having placed Alfred and Ruby in a class of their own, let us now look at some other pioneers, one of the most important of whom was Dr. Hilary James, a psychotherapist at the Middlesex Hospital. Dr. James had always been very interested in good food and, while still a medical student, had been famous among his friends for his excellent cooking. After he had qualified and begun to practise, he found that he was not satisfied with the London restaurant scene; he did not like the food, the service, waiters in dirty tail-coats nor the necessity for customers to dress up if they wanted to go to a restaurant. He had become very fond of the little informal restaurants in the South of France which offered very good food in an atmosphere devoid of any pretentions and so, egged on by the enthusiastic encouragement of his friends, he decided to open a restaurant of his own. In 1952 he opened Le Matelot in Elizabeth Street and, while continuing with his psychotherapy work during the day, he cooked at the restaurant in the evenings. The staff was so small that one evening, soon after the opening, when one of them was ill, the restaurant had to close. But he was helped by many of his friends working as waiters and washers-up on a casual basis and later he did employ a chef whom he taught to cook in his own way. From the start, both customers and waiters dressed informally and it always amused him when customers could not work out who was a fellow-diner and who was a waiter!

At first the cooking was quite simple, but it gradually developed with some influence from Elizabeth David, whose books Dr. James read with enthusiasm. The specialities included *escargots, coquilles St. Jacques* and *Scampi Provencal en brochette*. Being a great lover of wine, Dr. James always offered a good list and tried to mark up prices as little as he could afford.

From its opening night, Le Matelot was a huge success; so much so in fact that the proprietor had to open another restaurant almost next door in 1954 to help absorb some of the customers that Le Matelot had to turn away every evening. This second restaurant was called La Bicyclette and at first it offered very much the same food and *ambiance* as Le Matelot though it had its own speciality: chicken in the basket with sweet-corn pancakes. Later it was redecorated and began to offer more ambitious food created by Ray Parkes, who came to be recognized as one of the greatest chefs of the century.

One of the secrets of Dr. James's success was that whenever there was a staff shortage in one of his restaurants he could, and often did, stand-in in almost any capacity. At different times he played the role of chef, waiter and washer-up and thus ensured that no member of his staff was completely indispensable.

Though it is not strictly relevant, I cannot resist recounting here Dr. James's happiest moment as a *restaurateur*. The incident occurred at his third restaurant, the Forge, at Plaxtol in Kent. One evening he had some particularly difficult customers who were complaining about everything and they began to depress both the staff and all the other diners. Finally they said that their chicken dish was made of rabbit. Dr. James respectfully pointed out that it would have been an anatomical impossibility to fit some of the bones on their plate on to a rabbit's skeleton, but the diners would not listen. Then, remembering an idea of Clement Freud's, Dr. James whispered to his staff and at an agreed signal they all swooped on the table and removed everything that was on it.

'But my wife has not finished her coffee,' protested the rude diner.

'That's all right, you will not have to pay for it, in fact you will not have to pay for anything at all. You can go on sitting here if you wish but I suggest you go away and never, never return.'

31. Bill Stoughton at the Hungry Horse.

Everyone in the restaurant was glad to see them go and the whole evening continued in a jolly party atmosphere.

At about the same time as Dr. James opened La Bicyclette, Bill Stoughton left the Watergate Theatre Club and took the lease of a little antique shop in Walton Street which, with the aid of a partner, he transformed into La Popote. Stoughton had realized that it was a time when people were beginning to buy smaller houses or flats and a time when many of those who had been used to having staff were managing without. They would therefore want to eat out more than previously and they would want to have local eating-houses which they could use without having to dress up. The thinking was good and, thanks to the enthusiastic write-up which La Popote received from the numerous members of the Press who had regularly enjoyed Stoughton's cooking at the Watergate, the restaurant was fully booked every night from the opening onwards.

For some time Stoughton did all the cooking himself and one of the dishes which quickly became famous was Scampi Bill. He based the idea for this dish on something he had enjoyed at Wheeler's in Old Compton Street, but he incorporated some of his own imagination into it as well. The scampi were blanched, then some of the liquid from the blanching was put into a *béchamel* to which white wine and cream was added. Finally they were sprinkled with cheese and put under the grill. Another favourite was Chicken Popote which was served on rice with a sauce of white wine, white grapes, and pimentos. He also enjoyed making a *bisque* of squid scampi and other seafood.

Stoughton says he is amazed that no one had tried to introduce this style of restaurant and this style of cooking before. He claims that even in the 1930s enough people had discovered the little restaurants in the South of France which Dr. James loved so dearly, to have made it worth while trying to open such a place in London. But no one did.

La Popote's clientele in the early days was probably far more mixed than it is now. Young people were just beginning to have money and they were therefore present in quite large numbers, but there were not enough of them to support the restaurant on their own. It was some years before it became primarily a young people's restaurant, though even today there is still a sprinkling of older people.

While the various pioneers of 'amusing' food that I have mentioned were busy opening their special kind of restaurants, another man who is regarded today as one of the most significant names in British gastronomy, tried a different sort of experiment. In 1952 he opened a small, cosy restaurant in Hans Road called the Marquee where the highest possible standard of French cuisine was offered. His name was Egon Ronay.

At that time *haute cuisine* was only found in the famous large restaurants of London, such as the Caprice, the Coq d'or and the Ecu de France. The idea of dining out in Chelsea would never have occurred to the *habitués* of these places. The only part of London where small restaurants offering a high standard were to be found was Soho but, in any case, that was rather a different scene.

Looking back on his efforts at the Marquee, Ronay says rather sadly that he was ten years too early – at that time the people who were in a position to afford French *haute cuisine* simply did not go out to small restaurants and so

32. Egon Ronay.

the Marquee was financially un-rewarding. But Ronay had his rewards in other ways – the Press hailed it as 'the most food-perfect restaurant in London'. How was this achieved?

Before opening the Marquee, Ronay had worked as manager of an exclusive night-club called Ninety-Six Piccadilly, and while in that post he had brought to England an outstanding chef, a man who had previously been chef at the Metropole Hotel at Beaulieu. This man, with Ronay's inspiration, built up the superb repertoire of dishes at the Mar-quee and he insisted that every-thing, including soups, should be freshly cooked to order. Their specialities included *Sole au Plat Joinville* which was served with a white wine, mushroom, and shrimp sauce, *Bouillabaisse*, sliced duckling in orange and curaçao sauce and *Poulet Piperade*, that is, chicken with pimentos, tomatoes, and chopped bacon. The whole restaurant was most attractively decorated, so that one felt that one was inside an actual marquee and it is a tragedy that its character was completely changed as soon as Ronay sold it in 1955.

To return to what we are calling 'amusing food', the Harrington Hotel opened a small basement restaurant in the early 1950s which was the first French '*bistro*' in London. Most of the staff were French, the waitresses being students hoping to improve their English, and the food was all reliable *bourgeois* French cuisine. The décor was very simple but its red and white check table-cloths gave it an air of authenticity.

In 1955 a novelist called Walter Baxter published two books, one with a homosexual theme and one with a heterosexual theme. Unfortunately they were considered a little *avant-garde* and so Baxter was taken to court accused of obscene libel. Eventually both he and his publisher were acquitted, but the whole experience left Baxter feeling shattered and he decided that if he

33. Walter Baxter at the Chanterelle.

could not write what he wanted to write, it was no good going on as a novelist. What, then, was he to do? The only subject he really knew anything about and that he had always been interested in, was food. His father owned a firm which made sausages and so he had been brought up in an atmosphere where food was often a subject of conversation and had developed a taste for slightly unusual dishes like oxtail, sweetbread, calf's foot and so on. Also, during the war he had some quite interesting gastronomic experiences while serving as A.D.C. to Field-Marshal Slim. For a while he had to run the army commander's mess in Bengal, and this was a difficult job because most of the mess genuinely liked to eat spam and processed cheese and he had to teach them to enjoy the splendid vegetables, prawns and various kinds of fish that he was able to buy locally.

His experiences and his enthusiasm later made him decide that the best thing he could do would be to open a restaurant and so he started the Chanterelle in Old Brompton Road. He had one piece of luck, for at just the time he was looking round for a chef, Ray Parkes, whom Baxter had come to know through Dr. James, decided that he wanted to change his job and so became chef at the Chanterelle. It is a tribute to Parkes's genius that a number of the dishes which he created at the Chanterelle are still on the menu. His specialities included his famous garlic bread which has since been copied by a great many other establishments. Another speciality was *demi poussin* in cream and brandy with asparagus. To make this, half a chicken was placed in a pan with some asparagus on top of it and then a piece of Gruyère cheese was placed on the very top. In the oven, the cheese melted over the asparagus and kept them both moist and properly in position. When it was ready, it was taken out and a sauce of brandy, cream, and mushrooms was poured over it. Parkes loved frequently changing the menu, and other early favourites included sucking-pig, Pacific prawns grilled in their shells, and chicken cooked in butter and rosemary.

Like his friend Dr. James, Baxter was an enthusiastic reader of Elizabeth David and a number of her dishes found their way on to the menu of the Chanterelle, one of the most successful of which was *noisettes de porc à la Touraine* – that is: baked fillet of pork served with prunes and cream.

The Chanterelle was an immediate success. Baxter, who, as he says, comes from an ordinary middle-class background, knew very well what he liked to eat and what he liked to pay for it and so his tastes in food and prices were reflected in the clientele. They were mostly people in their thirties who, like so many of the customers of the other early 'amusing restaurants' had started going abroad either just before or after the war and who, on their return, were anxiously looking round for somewhere that served *aioli*.

Walter Baxter is the last of the pioneers I want to mention in the early 1950s and there can be no doubt that he, along with Alfred and Ruby, Bill Stoughton and Hilary James were the people who set a pattern which has been followed by countless others and transformed dining-out in London. Their followers and imitators opened numerous restaurants during the remainder of the decade, but I do not believe that they played a particularly significant part in the story of British gastronomy. I therefore intend to pass over them and, to complete the London scene of the 1950s, jump to 1959, that being the year when a particularly significant *restaurateur* opened his first establishment in London.

This *restaurateur* was educated at Eton and he had the misfortune to be there just after the war, when the school food was, even by Eton standards, particularly poor. Happily he had relatives in America who visited England from time to time, bringing with them food parcels for this under-nourished Etonian. These food parcels were the greatest thrill in life for Nicholas Clarke at that time and they gave him a consuming interest in manufactured food. He dreamed of what fun it would be if he could one day own a

34. Nick Clarke.

food factory. Nick did not work very hard at Eton and eventually this made his father concerned enough to send him off to take an aptitude test. The result of the test was sent in a report to Mr. Clarke senior, and it recommended that young Nick should go into the catering trade but, if possible, into some part of the trade that had a bit of 'show-biz' flavour about it.

The first proof of the accuracy of this test report came when Nick was appointed messing officer of his battalion during National Service and this interested him so much that, before leaving the Army, he wrote home to say that he had decided that, instead of trying to become a member of Lloyds, he would open a restaurant. In order to gain experience he spent the first eight months after National Service working in the kitchens of the Regent Palace Hotel and one or two other restaurants and coffee-bars. From there he drifted into 'public relations' and after changing jobs a few times he bought a house in Ifield Road, Chelsea, which had a transport café attached to it.

This was the time when Chelsea was first becoming what would now be called 'trendy' with a curious social mixture of people doing odd things. It was in the midst of this that Nick had first conceived the idea of running a workman's transport café and Ifield Road was almost perfect for him.

For the first six months he only served breakfasts and lunches. The lunch cost 17½p and consisted of 'dinner, sweet, and tea'. Then he decided to be a little more ambitious and so the café was given a proper restaurant menu in the evenings and its atmosphere was enhanced by candles being placed on the tables. Almost at once the Press discovered the Jekyll and Hyde nature of the restaurant and was thrilled with it and it quickly became such an outstanding success as 'Nick's Diner' that the transport-café side had to be dropped. In the early days Nick did much of the cooking himself – it was chiefly French *bourgeois* food and once again Elizabeth David's influence was much in evidence. Today it would be thought of as perfectly ordinary, but it would not be an exaggeration to say that it was sensational in 1959. Early favourites were *taramasalata*, *soupe à l'oignon*, home-made *pâté* and *terrine*, steak in various kinds of sauce and garlic potatoes. After the restaurant had been going for a while, Nick was introduced to a master-chef called Kem Bennett who raised the tone of the cuisine and the Diner became famous, among other things, for its individually cooked portions of *bœuf en croûte*, accompanied by a sort of *purée* of mushroom.

Nick's Diner was not, of course, the first *bistro* but it was early enough to have a profound effect on the numerous *bistros* that began to open in large numbers in the early sixties and it was ahead of its time in being one of the first places to offer 'a meal experience' – something that was in great demand in the sixties as we shall see in the next chapter.

While a small number of enlightened amateurs were thus busily at work making eating out more amusing and varied in London, a number of equally dedicated people, many of whom were also amateurs, were spreading the light of gastronomy in various places throughout the country where it had never shone before. There were not many good restaurants outside London in the 1950s, but then we must remember that until the 1950s eating outside London had been something of a penance.

I have no hesitation in saying that, with the possible exception of some of the establishments operated by that enlightened group, British Transport Hotels, the very first place to offer really imaginative and delicious food outside London was the Hole in the Wall at Bath, which was acquired in 1952 by George Perry-Smith.

George Perry-Smith is the most modest of *restaurateurs*, being a shy, retiring man. He is the son of a Nonconformist minister and so was brought up in a background where to talk of food at all was considered mildly irreverent. After leaving school he went to Cambridge and, while he was an undergraduate there, discovered the joys of cooking. Then the war came and he gained further culinary expertise in the catering department of the Society of Friends' Ambulance Service. This was especially useful, he says, in teaching him about the preparation and cooking of vegetables.

After the war he thought he would like to teach and his good degree in Modern Languages secured him a position as an *assistant d'Anglais* at the Lycée Saint-Louis in the Boulevard Saint-Michel in Paris. This post gave him the perfect opportunity to get to know many of the excellent little restaurants of the Left Bank and helped to widen his gastronomic horizon. Nevertheless, when he returned to England he decided to go on with academic work and so he took a post at a grammar school in Bristol. Common-room life, with all its internal politics and tricky relationships, was not well suited to a sensitive person like George Perry-Smith so he left and began to look for 'a job that both gave me the opportunity to use my hands and the opportu-

35. George Perry-Smith.

nity to be nice to people'. After a while it occurred to him that these two qualities were potentially to be found in the vocation of *restaurateur* and so, with his £2,000 capital, he started to look round for suitable premises. Soon he found a rather disreputable restaurant called the Hole in the Wall at Bath. He is not quite sure what made it unsalubrious, but thinks it was something to do with the fact that it had an all-night licence. He bought the restaurant and quickly set about changing its reputation.

The Hole in the Wall remained closed while Perry-Smith and a particularly helpful Non-conformist builder-cum-architect worked frantically to transform the place in such a way as to provide a sympathetic and un-obtrusive background in which his excellent food could be served.

Just before the building operations were complete, Perry-Smith was fortunate enough to secure the services of a former officer in the Royal Canadian Mounted Police as his chef. His name was Christopher Hammond-Spencer, and he and his wife, together with a French waiter called Alexei, comprised the entire staff. This was a time when the menu of almost any reasonably respectable restaurant outside London read something like this:

Brown Windsor Soup
or
Cream of Tomato

Roast Chicken and Bread Sauce
or
Steak and Kidney pudding
or
Silverside of Beef with boiled carrots

Stewed Rhubarb and custard
or
Apple Pie and cream

Very nice – but how dull to come across this for the thousandth time. Perry-Smith's menu at the time of opening in 1952 was so utterly different and so amazingly imaginative for its time that I have decided to reproduce it here in full:

HORS-D'ŒUVRE

Canapés	Anchovies
Charcuterie	Pâté en croûte
Sea Food	Foie gras
Egg Dishes	Salads
Blinis and Caviare	

SOUPS

Pea Soup (Navy fashion)	Game Soup
Tomato Soup	Scotch Broth
Vegetable Soups in season	Consommé

Continental and American Specialities:
Minestrone with Parmesan Cheese
Bouillabaisse (as nearly as possible)
Bisques
Fish Chowder
Bortsch (as nearly as possible)

OMELETTES and **EGGS** whenever we are allowed to serve them.

FISH

Grilled Dover Sole
Fried Fillets of Plaice
Grilled Herring
Soused Herring
Kedgeree
Creamed Mussels
Grilled steaks of Turbot or Halibut

Oysters
Dressed Crab
Shrimps
Smoked Salmon
Casserole of Fish
Lobster

Continental and American specialities:

Koulibiac

Lobster Newburg

MIXED GRILLS

Steak or Chop, Sausage, Bacon, Tomato, Mushroom,
Onions, French fried potatoes

ENTRÉES

Jugged Hare
Grilled Ham
Tripe and Onions
Spaghetti au gratin

Braised Rabbit
Curried Chicken and other
Curries
Cheese Tart

Pies – Rabbit, Beef and Kidney, Game and others

Continental and American Specialities:

Ravioli
Risotto
Hungarian Goulash
Chicken Maryland
Hamburger Steaks
Spaghetti and Macaroni dishes

Pork Chops and Country Gravy
Baked Beans – Boston style
Chili con carne
Quiche Lorraine
Vienna Schnitzel

ROASTS

Game and Poultry in season
Joints served on the table d'hôte menus

COLD BUFFET

Cold Ham and hot meats
Cold Game in season
Hunters' Beef
Salads and Pickles

Smoked Salmon
Sea Food in season
Cold Pies

VEGETABLES

Potatoes – boiled, roast, French fried, creamed,
scalloped, mashed, baked in their jackets
Green and root vegetables in season

SALADS

Green salads in season
Tomatoes
Mixed 'American' salads

CHEESES

There will always be as wide a choice as possible from

Normandy Camembert	Brie
Port Salut	Roquefort
Pont l'Evêque	Carré de l'est
Bleu d'Auvergne	Danish Blue Vein
Gruyère	Gorgonzola
Stilton	Cheddar

Bread and Biscuits will be served as requested.

SWEETS

Sundaes	Pancakes
Ices	Waffles with syrup
Trifles	Fruit Shortcake
Meringues	Rum Baba
Rum Omelette	Tarts and Pastries
Fruit	

SAVOURIES

Cheese Aigrettes	Savoury Croûtes
Devils on Horseback	Canapés
Croque-Monsieur	Cheese Pastries
Epicure	

COFFEE

Twining's Blue Mountain Jamaica
Blue Danube Viennese
Turkish

TEA

Twining's Choice Fannings
Golden Tea-Tips
Pure China
Darjeeling and Lapsang Souchong

The waiter will be glad to tell you what other beverages are available.

The cooking was based on the Gloucester College of Science Cookery Book and on some of the early writings of Elizabeth David.

The restaurant was an enormous success from the start – people were delighted with the completely new experience that a visit to the Hole in the Wall provided. Bath was the ideal place in which to start such a restaurant because it was full of retired people, many of whom had acquired a taste for foreign cooking before the war. Also, many of the visitors to the town were rather better-off potential *bon viveurs*. The only disadvantage was that Perry-Smith was not able to obtain a licence for some time so that customers either had to bring their own wine or send a waiter out to Sainsbury's off-licence to buy some.

Perry-Smith supposed at the time of opening that a large number of his customers would demand plain steaks and fried fish but this was not, in fact, the case. Only a very small minority ever failed to be tempted by the rather more exotic masterpieces that abounded on his menu.

After the restaurant had been running for a few months, Hammond-Spencer found the strain of cooking for the large *à la carte* menu was too great and decided to retire but, happily, the restaurant did not suffer from this as he had been able to pass his knowledge on to Perry-Smith. Indeed, one of the strong points of the Hole in the Wall has always been that it is so consistent. Its character and menu scarcely changed at all in the twenty years that Perry-Smith owned it – a tribute to the sound thinking behind it at the start.

One particularly outstanding feature of the Hole in the Wall has always been its cold table, and this was something that Perry-Smith particularly enjoyed preparing. Never were different kinds of vegetable served together with a single dressing – each vegetable was given its own individual treatment. Typical dishes included various types of *pâté* (both of meat and of fish), mussels, mushrooms, broccoli, egg dishes, tomatoes stuffed with *taramasalata*, onions in soured cream, one or two rice dishes, aubergines, pimentos, a *quiche* of some sort and a cold pie.

George Perry-Smith has influenced virtually every successful *restaurateur* in the whole country outside London. In many cases his staff have gone on to open restaurants of their own having learned by observation. What, then, were the guiding principles that motivated him?

First, he felt that a restaurant should have a minimum of *chi-chi*. He considered a relaxed atmosphere to be of paramount importance and sought to provide a haven of peace into which customers could escape from the roar of traffic outside. Secondly, he considered it most important that his customers should be received with a smile and genuine friendliness and that they should be made to feel that the restaurant is theirs.

He therefore never tried to influence his customers' choice of food or wine and sometimes felt at a loss for ideas when asked about what he would recommend. Finally, I would say that he is an extraordinary combination of amateurishness, casualness, and great professionalism – in other words he does everything in the right way without losing even a little of his humanity.

Perry-Smith really had no direct rivals for many years, but to give justice where it is due, there were, in the 1950s, just a handful of other country restaurants where the standard was well above average and one of the most important of these was the Bell at Aston Clinton.

The Bell has been an inn since the 18th century but it only became widely known after 1940 because that was the year in which it was acquired by Gerard Harris. Harris was a successful solicitor in London during the 1930s, but when the war came and his wife was pregnant, they decided that the best thing for him to do would be to find a new home and a new job outside London. The Bell provided him with both and so he duly signed an agreement with the brewery who owned it and became the licensee (he bought it from the brewery, in 1953).

Soon Harris developed a personal philosophy: in his old job as a solicitor people had come to him chiefly when they were in trouble; now he wanted them to come to him to enjoy themselves. Obviously the right way to help them in this respect was to offer them the highest possible standard of food and wine. Harris was in a good position to do this as he was himself a *bon viveur* and, perhaps inspired by caring for the legal problems of two firms in the wine trade, had built up a very fine cellar of his own which he brought with him to the Bell.

Inevitably it was not all plain sailing in the early days. The manager's sobriety could not always be counted upon and the kitchen roof was in such a bad state of repair that the chef, Frank Green, had to set up umbrellas there on rainy days. Green does seem to have been very hardy, for in addition to coping with the leaking roof, he bicycled the ten miles from his home at Quainton to Aston Clinton every day and in all weathers without a murmur of complaint.

In the early days of Harris's régime the food was exceptionally good but simple. The specialities were Aylesbury duckling, steak and kidney pudding, and *Bœuf Avignon* which was a form of *Bœuf Bourguignonne*. After the war Harris began to travel abroad at regular intervals and so the menu became far more varied – indeed the Bell was one of the first provincial restaurants to offer snails. He also began to build up his cellar so that the already excellent

1. The Café Royal in the 1890s

2. The Horn of Plenty, Gulworthy, in the Spring

wine list grew and grew. At the time of writing, Michael Harris (Gerard's son) has no less than 80,000 bottles.

One of the other good country restaurants in the 1950s was the Miners' Arms at Priddy in Somerset. In the 18th century, the Miners' Arms was a wayside inn frequented by men working in the local lead mines and by travellers. In the latter part of the century lead mining was given up for a time but, with the arrival of new techniques, was revived in the early 19th century and continued right up until 1906. But trade did not fall off completely after 1906 as the inn was frequented by sheep drovers, the Mendip Hills being an important area for wool at that time. It was also a centre for the large number of poachers who thrived in that part of Somerset early in this century and, because of this, a local landowner appealed to the magistrates to withdraw its licence in 1913. The licence was withdrawn and from that time on it was run at various times as a café, a guest-house, and even as a residential riding-school. Then, in 1954, it was acquired by a research fellow of Bristol University called Hywell Murrell who wanted to use it both as his home and as a guest-house. As Murrell's wife was more interested in painting and art than in cooking, they found a retired Colonel called House to run the culinary side of the business. Colonel House was very enthusiastic about good food and had acquired a little practical experience while helping a friend to run a pub. It was not long before the cooking at the Miners' Arms under his régime became famous in the district and from 1958, when it first appeared in the *Good Food Guide*, it has had a reputation throughout the country.

The Miners' Arms really is just about the most unlikely place in which to find a good restaurant – it is a small, ordinary-looking white house in the middle of nowhere and it has no visible sign on the outside to inform potential customers of its existence. Nevertheless, for those who are clever enough to find it, a remarkably varied and imaginative menu is available and a fine selection of wines. It did not take long for Murrell and Colonel House to convince magistrates that the restoration of the licence would not lead to the reappearance of the poachers, but there was still a problem inasmuch as there is no cellar at the Miners' Arms. Happily, Priddy is not too far from Bristol and so an arrangement was made with Averys whereby their wines could be kept in Bristol and small quantities would be brought as required to replenish the modest stock kept at the restaurant. In this way it was possible to offer a good selection of wines and to ensure that they were in perfect condition.

In some ways conditions at the restaurant were a little primitive at that

time – they could not easily serve either aperitives or after-dinner drinks –
but the high standard of cooking and the wine list ensured that no one
regretted going there. Here are some examples of dishes offered there in
1958:

Home-made *pâté*
(i) liver, onion, tomato, and tarragon
(ii) liver, ham, onion, and mushroom
(iii) liver, cider, paprika, gin, and thyme
(iv) duck liver, with brandy and sherry
(v) terrine of liver veal and bacon

Chicken
(i) with olives
(ii) with onion, tomato, and white wine
(iii) casseroled with onion, green peppers, carrots, and garlic
(iv) smothered with cream, onions, and white wine
(v) with mushrooms and cider

Steak *au cognac*
Steak with onion and herbs sauce or with Madeira sauce

Duck in orange sauce with Curaçao

Veal steak in Madeira sauce

Among the puddings was 'Miners' Delight', a dish which is still available
today. If I describe it to you, it will sound terrible and put you off. In fact it
is delicious, so it is worth going there and trying it.

Colonel House retired in 1958 but the high standards he had set were
continued under his successors until 1961, when the Miners' Arms was
acquired by Mr. and Mrs. Paul Leyton who raised the gastronomic tone
still further, as we shall see in the next chapter.

Chapter 5

RECENT YEARS

THE beginning of the 1960s is a good moment at which to pause and reflect on the achievements of the post-war recovery period. One of those who did this at the time was Raymond Postgate who had this to say in his tenth *Good Food Guide* which came out in 1961:

> If the decennial period is considered as a whole . . . moderate congratulation on our progress is permissible. In other words, food in Britain is nothing like as bad as it was ten or so years ago. But then, it was intolerable in those days. There is still a lot of dreadful food served in this island, but at that time there was practically nothing else at all but dreadful food. One had to single out for praise places where a joint and two veg. were merely edible, and the staff were neither too obviously incompetent nor unbearably rude. . . . As for materials, butter was never used in cooking, it was always marge. Cream was never real cream; it was a sort of sweetened white grease offered under one of various fancy names. From the Argentine to the Cape the world was combed to secure for us the worst cuts of the most elderly and stringy cows and ewes. That has changed. Materials are better and more abundant, and though, in roughly half the establishments in this country, the cooking is as bad as it was then, in the other half it isn't.

Progress, indeed, but not without a little regression too, for, as Postgate went on to say, by 1961 although greater care was being taken with the grilling of steaks and the roasting of chickens, the quality of the raw material was not always better – there simply was not enough Angus beef for all the restaurants that claimed to serve it and the battery chickens which were becoming popular at about that time were no real substitute for free-range ones.

Nevertheless the sixties were, for the most part, years of progress. In London they saw the 'amusing' restaurants of the 1950s reach their peak and the birth of a small number of outstandingly good new restaurants of a more serious nature while eating out in the provinces at last became a real pleasure. By the end of the decade, there were good restaurants, usually run by a *chef-patron*, in most parts of England and in many parts of Scotland. Wales also had begun to enjoy more serious cooking in such places as the

Walnut Tree Inn at Llandewi Skirrid and a start had been made in Northern Ireland.

Let us begin by looking at the 'amusing' restaurants in London. Nick Clarke who, as we have seen, was proprietor of one of the restaurants in this category had this to say: 'The sixties was a period when people were very sensation-hungry and this was caused by the fact that many people, especially the young, had money for the first time and did not know exactly how to spend it, as they had not been brought up in a rich tradition. They therefore began to go to untraditional places such as boutiques and trendy hair-dressers.' Restaurateuring is, Nick says, in a sense part of the entertainment industry and people like him are selling a 'meal experience', a combination of amusing waiters, original décor and imaginative cooking. As people's lives become tenser and more exacting than ever before, so they long, when they go out, to escape from all that concerns them in the ordinary way. They do not just want to go out to save the wife toiling over a hot stove, they want to be transported into a sort of fairyland where they are pleased, cosseted, and excited.

I am sure that Mr. Clarke is absolutely correct in this analysis and the general pattern of London restaurants in the 1960s reflected this. More and more places began to open with 'way-out' decorations and theatrical atmospheres. There was a great 'trattoria' boom during which large numbers of Italian restaurants sprouted all over London offering what Osbert Lancaster called 'King's Road Mediterranean'. These were successful for very much the same reason – that they transported people out of their everyday lives, recalled exciting and romantic moments on holidays abroad and so, naturally, people flocked to them. The only trouble was that very often the restaurateurs who opened all these 'meal experience' places did not care as much about the food they served as the atmosphere in which they served it. Of course there were many exceptions, like Nick Clarke's 'diner' and some of the trattorias opened by Mario and Franco, where a real effort was made with the food, but I believe that there was only one restaurant in London which combined an extraordinary atmosphere and décor with truly outstanding cooking and that was Parkes', in Beauchamp Place.

Ray Parkes was an astonishing person and Egon Ronay was not exaggerating when he said recently, 'I think Ray Parkes is absolutely unique in the history of British catering, he was a genius – he was a true creator of dishes such as has never existed before.' Parkes began by training to be an architect at the Leeds School of Architecture where he studied from 1946 to 1949. When he left, he decided to go into catering instead of architecture and so

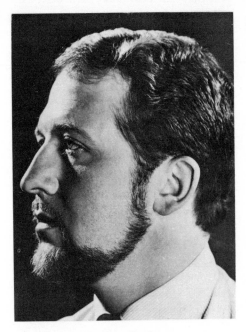

36. Ray Parkes.

joined forces with a friend in running the St. Mary's Hotel in York. Three years later the partnership came to an end and so Parkes, who had by this time come to realize that he had a definite gift for cooking, came down to London and, over a period of years, worked for the Wheelers group at the Carafe in Lowndes Street, for Dr. Hilary James at La Bicyclette and for Walter Baxter at the Chanterelle. During the time that he was working in these various places a certain Beecher Moore came to admire his cooking and followed him to whatever restaurant he was working at. After a while, Moore offered Parkes the use of his £750 capital if ever he wanted to set up a restaurant of his own. Parkes expressed some interest, but then someone else made a more substantial offer and he accepted that. However, he found it impossible to work with his new partner because he, Parkes, had very extravagant ideas about using expensive ingredients while his partner was more concerned with making a large profit. Eventually they split up; Parkes joined forces with Beecher Moore and Parkes' Restaurant opened in November 1960 in a former vet's surgery in Beauchamp Place. Because of the cramped premises they were at first obliged to call themselves a snack-bar to comply with the law but it certainly must have been the only snack-bar in London to serve chicken stuffed with lobster!

From the outset the restaurant pursued a number of unusual policies: it was among the first to give the host of each party a priced menu and his guests unpriced ones. Actually it is a habit I abhor but that is beside the point and they defend it by saying that it is only in this way that many excellent but cheaper dishes ever come to be chosen. Another more significant idea was to put totally incomprehensible but highly amusing names to the dishes on the menu and train the waiters to recite the explanations of the dishes to the customers. This was done to try and make people more adventurous in their choices and the system worked well. Some of the early specialities included 'Utter Bliss' – melon filled with raspberries or straw-

37. The Kitchen at Parkes' Restaurant.

berries; 'Ugly, Ugly Duckling' – half duckling surrounded with peaches, chestnuts, and apricots; 'Sweet, Sweet Mystery' – sweetbreads *en croûte*, and 'Some Like it Hot' – a Mexican soup made of avocados, tomatoes, and peppers.

Another tradition of the restaurant from the earliest days was to serve food with flowers. The reason for this was that Parkes, master-chef though he was, did not feel that food should be taken *too* seriously, nor could he guarantee that every single mouthful ever eaten in his restaurant would be perfection. His aim was to offer good food in a pleasant atmosphere and he felt that the flowers helped it all to be more fun and more relaxed.

Ray Parkes died in 1963 and sadly he left no written accounts of the dishes he created. Everyone who knew him was amazed by the way in which original ideas continued to flow from him and it is for this reason that many experts today rate him almost on a par with the chef that he himself admired most, Fernand Point of the Restaurant de la Pyramide at Vienne.

Not long after opening the restaurant, Parkes took on a former dry-cleaning engineer called Tom Benson as a washer-up. Soon realizing that Benson was a man of ability, Parkes made him his personal assistant and so Benson became his only pupil and for some years after his death did all the cooking at the restaurant. But he admits that he has never been able to cook exactly as Parkes did because his was such an instinctive and personal technique and so Parkes' genius is, in a sense, lost for ever and only lives on in the memories of those who knew him and had the privilege of enjoying his culinary masterpieces.

A number of people tried to copy Parkes's style of cooking and his style of restaurant but they were all such pale imitations of the original that we must pass over them and come to some of the more serious restaurants that opened in London in the 1960s. Of course, the old-established ones such as Prunier's, the Mirabelle, the Caprice and the Coq d'Or continued to flourish but I believe that the real leaders of gastronomic progress in London in recent years have been Rudolph Richard of the Connaught Hotel, Robert Carrier, Albert Roux of Le Gavroche and Le Poulbot, and David Levin of the Capital Hotel. In passing, it is interesting to note that two of these four are hotel keepers. Their achievement is all the greater since the general trend has been in favour of restaurants that are not attached to hotels.

Rudolph Richard was born in Switzerland in 1898 and learned the art of hotel management in various hotels abroad before coming to the Carlton Hotel in London. From there he went on to the Stafford Hotel and then spent some years in Gibraltar

38. Rudolph Richard.

where the Marquess of Bute had asked him to open the Rock Hotel. Then, in 1935, he was appointed manager of the Connaught Hotel which was so different then from what it is today that Richard's work in transforming it can only be described as astonishing.

Almost all the business came from families with permanent suites; they treated the hotel as their town house and were surprised if they came across casual visitors staying there. The homely atmosphere, naturally enough, extended to the dining-room where each table traditionally belonged to one particular family and where bottles of pills were often left on the tables to remind those with imperfect health that the 'three times a day after meals' rule should not be broken. Although trade in mineral waters was quite brisk, little wine was called for and *apéritifs* and *digestifs* were very rarely ordered. In the evening the dining-room closed at nine o'clock, after which residents could only obtain sandwiches and hot *consommé* from the night porter.

No doubt Richard must have dreamed, from the moment he took up his appointment at the Connaught, of making it into one of the greatest hotels in the world but he had to respect the wishes of the families who regularly visited it and would not have been at all pleased to find too many changes taking place. He therefore spent the years leading up to the war making very unostentatious but significant changes. He began to build up the cellar which, at the time of his arrival, was small and contained little of any interest and, by revealing his enthusiasm for and interest in good food to the kitchen staff, he gradually began to raise the standard of cuisine.

It was the war that really opened the way for Richard to transform the hotel. As I have said, he would never have wanted to make changes that might have upset his regular customers but the advent of war caused them to give up their permanent suites and retreat to the country and so he had to find new customers. The hotel thus came to be used by many foreign delegations visiting London during the war and its prestige was greatly enhanced when General de Gaulle made it his London headquarters. It was also during the war that the restaurant first began to attract non-residents in considerably greater numbers, especially Americans from the Embassy in Grosvenor Square and, in spite of rationing, the Connaught was able to feed them quite well because Richard applied his skill and energy in helping the chefs to make the very best possible use of such ingredients as were available.

By the end of the war, the Connaught had acquired quite a reputation as a very civilized hotel with an increasingly popular restaurant. By 1952 it was already the gastronomic equal of most of the great hotels of London and the *Good Food Guide* of that year reported: 'Exceptionally good international cooking in the atmosphere of a comfortable Edwardian hotel'. It also enthused over the restaurant's three great specialities, which it considered to be unique: *Crêpes de Volaille Connaught*, *Sole Carlos* and *Oeufs Pochés en surprise*. 'Despite high prices it is usually crowded and it is as well to telephone. There is a wine list of over 100 items, all but one (Beaujolais '49 for 85p) over £1 including some very interesting items such as Chateau Pavie 1924 (£2·25) and magnums of Chateau La Mission Haut Brion 1945 (£3).'

The transformation was already remarkable but Richard was determined to go a long way further.

In 1953, pressure for table reservations from non-residents was becoming so great that Simmons, the under-manager of the restaurant, suggested to Richard that a grill room should be created in a back room which was very rarely used and which had to be entered through a service pantry. The idea was quickly approved and after some complex work had been carried out to give the back room a proper entrance, to install bay windows and lower the ceiling, the Connaught Grill opened in May 1955.

The cooking and the wine list at the Connaught improved steadily during the fifties and the early sixties and there was still further progress when Daniel Dunas was appointed chef in 1965. Dunas served his apprentice-

39. Daniel Dunas in the kitchens of the Connaught Hotel.

ship in Chartres from 1945 to 1948 and thereafter cooked first in a private house in Paris and then for the American Embassy there. The next few years were spent at the American Embassy in Cairo and then he became a *commis* chef at Blenheim Palace. After a couple of years as pastry chef to the Governor-General in Ottawa he returned to Blenheim as head chef in 1956, where he remained until shortly before taking up his appointment at the Connaught.

Dunas and Richard worked in perfect harmony together. 'Mr. Richard', said Dunas, 'always wanted the best, anything that was an improvement always received his approval, he never refused me anything and that made my work much easier.' In return for all the help and encouragement he received from Richard, Dunas applied himself with the utmost determination and enthusiasm. He introduced a number of new specialities such as *Truite au Riesling*, which is a boiled river trout stuffed with a *mousseline* of sole with truffles, then cooked in Riesling and served with a cream and Riesling sauce. Another example is *Suprême de Volaille Marquise* – a chicken breast larded and cooked in butter then served with a green sauce made of asparagus and brandy.

Dunas's years with the Duke of Marlborough have made him one of the leading experts in cooking game and his English specialities, one of which is offered every day at the Connaught, are outstanding (only Friday being not strictly English though English in spirit).

DAILY SPECIALITIES AT THE CONNAUGHT

Monday:	Steak and kidney pie
Tuesday:	Irish stew
Wednesday:	Roast beef and Yorkshire pudding
Thursday:	Boiled silverside of beef and dumplings
Friday:	Salmon Koulibiac or oxtails
Saturday:	Steak and kidney pudding with mushrooms
Sunday:	Roast beef or chicken pie

In 1972 a very proud moment for Dunas came when one of his sous-chefs, who had been in effect his pupil, won the Pierre Taittinger Award – a prize for which over 100 chefs from all over the world had competed. His dish is really too complicated to describe but suffice it to say that spinach, sole and crayfish tails could never be made into anything more exquisite!

Rudolph Richard died on 12 June 1973 and his death was mourned all

over the world. His influence had extended to hotels in Cape Town and
Madeira and, of course, to Paris where he was chairman of the Lancaster
Hotel. But it was above all for the Connaught that he cared and he devoted
to it all his skill, energy, and enthusiasm. It was well known that his most
thrilling moment came when he arrived at a London station, told a taxi-
driver to take him to the Connaught and for the first time did not have to
explain where it was.

A gastronomic giant of a very different sort is Robert Carrier and I have
chosen my words well, for he is a large man as well as being one of the most
important leaders of the culinary and restaurant worlds that England has
ever known. Perhaps the most extraordinary thing about him is that he
just drifted into being a food writer and *restaurateur* without ever really
intending to do so, in rather the same way as Marcel Boulestin did just after
the First World War.

Carrier was born in America of a German mother and Irish father and
first found that he had a gift for cooking at the age of four: 'I made a fried
egg sandwich and gave it to one of my friends. He talked about it so much
the rest of the gang wanted one. I knew I was on to a good thing.' However,
he had to wait a long time before any further significant progress was made.
The next stage came when he spent six years in Paris, beginning in the
latter part of the war, working as a journalist and broadcaster. Paris filled
him with a very deep love of good cooking but, at the time his work came
to an end there, he still had little practical knowledge of how to cook.
The groundwork of this knowledge was put in during a period of eighteen
months which he spent in St. Tropez recovering from hepatitis. During
the time when he was actually suffering from the disease, his diet was restricted to carrot soup and to compensate for the frustration of existing on such
dull fare he began to read every cookery book he could lay hands on.
Then, in St. Tropez, when he was beginning to feel better he began to
learn to cook from a friend of his called Fifine, the proprietor of a restaurant
there. But Carrier only did this cooking for fun and as a sort of therapy.
As soon as he was really fit and well again he went in for acting and when
that proved unsuccessful moved on to public relations. The acting period
was a useful one in widening his gastronomic horizons as his company went
on tour in Italy and this gave him a splendid opportunity to sample the
cuisine of all the regions of Italy.

Carrier's P.R. work was also useful in providing him with some further
gastronomic experience, as his most important accounts included the pro-
motion of apples on behalf of five countries, cornflour and corn-oil. To

40. Robert Carrier.

stimulate interest in these products he wrote articles describing exciting dishes which used these ingredients and offered them to women's magazines and any other journals that were interested, together with mouth-watering coloured photographs. Through the library of cookery books, which he had by this time collected, he discovered that 97 per cent of all Chinese recipes use corn-starch or cornflour, so he learned to cook Chinese food and gave a giant four-hour banquet for the Press at which he taught them to eat with chopsticks. He followed this up by sending out Chinese recipes to many national newspapers and periodicals and most of them were published. The result was that his sponsors were well pleased with him.

It was probably as a result of these promotional efforts that *Harpers Bazaar* came to hear of him and when they invited him to write a food article for them in September 1958, he jumped at the idea. He says it was the worst article he ever wrote but *Harpers* liked it, as did their readers, and soon he was asked to produce some more articles for them. It was not long before he became an established feature of the magazine. Other appointments swiftly followed: in 1961 he left *Harpers* to become food editor of *Vogue* and in 1963, while still working for *Vogue*, he became the first food editor of the *Sunday Times Magazine*. In the midst of all this he still found time to do his P.R. work and to produce his cookery cards and two of the very first cookery books to reach the best-seller class. Naturally enough, many people approached him and asked him to run a restaurant for them, but he resisted their offers until finally he agreed to join a group which included Harry Secombe and Frank Sinatra and together they opened the Pickwick Club. Carrier's job was to make the food good and to train the chefs in his ways of cooking. He did succeed in doing this but not before the chefs had left him high and dry for a while to do all the cooking almost single-handed.

Carrier's efforts in the kitchens of the Pickwick Club made him feel, when he left it after six months or so, that he would like to own a restaurant himself and so, when one day he and his accountant were walking down Camden Passage on the way to his home in Islington and he noticed a little restaurant was up for sale, he said 'If that's cheap enough, buy it'. It was cheap enough and he did buy it with the intention of offering it to his valet Yanni and Yanni's wife Stephania to run it for him. They had learned to cook very competently while in his employment so he was sure that they were equal to the task. Unfortunately, these two enthusiastic Greeks were so upset when they heard that Carrier would not allow them to start serving meals until the restaurant had been redecorated and re-equipped, that they left and went home to Greece. Carrier thus found himself with no staff and with a restaurant on his hands and so decided to make a go of it himself. He had the restaurant beautifully decorated and then, a few weeks before it was complete, he hired a sous-chef from the Savoy who promised to bring a first-class *pâtissier* along with him. He also hired a local grill-chef.

Three days before opening, while he was hanging the curtains and while there was no sign outside, a journalist from *The Times* arrived in Camden Passage and asked Carrier if she could come along for lunch on the next day. He said 'yes' and after the meal she was so thrilled with the cooking that she came back with a photographer. The result was that a large article with pictures appeared in *The Times* on the opening day calling the restaurant 'Carrier's' and praising it to the skies. They had to turn away almost eighty people a day for the first three months! In fact the opening night turned out to be something of a nightmare for Carrier since the sous-chef from the Savoy went into hospital on that afternoon and on hearing this news, his friend the *pâtissier* decided not to turn up either. Quite by chance a man popped into the restaurant early in the evening when Carrier and his grill-chef were wondering how on earth they would cope and said 'I'm a wonderful chef, is there any chance of a job?'

'You're hired', came the instantaneous reply.

The restaurant offers a fixed-price menu with a choice of about five dishes for each of the four courses. In addition to these there is a section called 'Great Dishes of the day' which are his *plats du jour* and a small selection of dishes using particularly expensive ingredients for which an extra charge is made. Carrier is, as everyone knows, a food enthusiast and he cannot bear the idea of people coming all the way to his restaurant and then only eating two non-fattening courses and a cup of coffee.

The menus are beautifully balanced to ensure that diners will not feel too uncomfortably full at the end of their meal. The first courses are delicious cold items such as French cucumber salad with fresh herbs and *pâté de canard en croûte*. This is then followed by a soup or perhaps something like his *délices au Gruyère* which he describes as 'creamy pillows of Gruyère and Parmesan deep-fried until crisp and golden and flavoured with freshly-grated Parmesan and paprika'.

Carrier's main courses always serve to remind one how international his knowledge of gastronomy is. On a typical day you might be invited to choose between a plain English dish like baby lamb chops with mint or a brochette of lamb with Moroccan spices (*hefla*, cummin and cayenne), a Greek *souvlaka* of Turbot or a classic French dish like *ris de veau à la crême*.

Even the vegetables are quite unlike those found anywhere else and are usually delicious. Carrier's carrots are poached in a lemon-flavoured sauce, his French beans are carefully cooked *al dente* and then finished in butter with herbs and his saffron rice with avocado is a splendid creation.

The puddings are usually the simplest part of the menu but even they are prepared with considerable imagination and there is often at least one pudding made from an ancient recipe such as Elizabeth Moxon's Lemon Posset. The lemon posset is a light foam of cream flavoured with white wine, lemon juice, and freshly grated lemon rind.

We will now leave Robert Carrier for the moment, though we shall have to come back to him later to look at his contribution to British provincial gastronomy, and turn to two brothers who are dedicated chefs: Albert and Michel Roux. Michel, the younger brother, began his training as a *pâtissier* at the age of fourteen and worked at the British Embassy in Paris and later for Rothschild's Bank in Paris. After his National Service he was appointed the youngest-ever personal chef to the Rothschild family at the age of twenty-two. Albert also worked at the British Embassy in Paris but before then, at the age of eighteen, he had come to England and worked for the Astors and the Clores. Then, after military service and his spell at the British Embassy, he spent nine years working for Peter Cazalet. Roux was very happy with the Cazalets, but, after several years in private service, he began to feel a desire to offer to the public at large the same very high standard of cooking that he was producing for his employer and a few privileged guests. Michel

41. Albert Roux after lunch at Le Poulbot.

also felt he would enjoy the opportunity of exposing his work to wider criticism and so, in 1967, with some financial help from the Cazalets and their friends, the two brothers opened Le Gavroche in Lower Sloane Street.

The restaurant had a very good start; eight ambassadors attended the opening dinner and for a while bookings could only be accepted for three months ahead and, as was well known at the time, even Princess Margaret was unable to book a table at shorter notice than that. Why all the fuss in a small and rather ordinary-looking restaurant with a tiled floor and closely-parked tables? The answer, of course, lies in the cooking. The Roux brothers produce classically-based French dishes with innovations of their own that are among the best in Britain. Their specialities include an exceptional cheese *soufflé* called *Soufflé Suissesse*, *Poulet Paulinette* which is a *poussin* completely de-boned and stuffed with a mousse of chicken and spring vegetables. The whole dish is then poached in a *consommé* with sherry and served with rice. Their *Homard à l'escargot* is a lobster that is plainly boiled and then taken out of its shell. The shell is then lined with butter and garlic after which the meat is put back in place. Finally the whole dish is baked in the oven and served with *béarnaise*.

The cold table at Le Gavroche is also outstanding and contains such items as *paupiettes de saumon Claudine*: wafer-thin slices of smoked salmon stuffed with a mousse made of smoked salmon and salmon trout, then glazed with jelly and decorated. The Crab *Vahinée* is a fresh crab that has been boiled and very thoroughly cleaned. The meat is returned to the shell where it rests on a bed of shallots, avocados, pimentos, and tabasco sauce.

After Le Gavroche had been open for a few months, more and more people began to ask the proprietors to open a comparable restaurant in the City. In 1969 they did so, and Le Poulbot in Cheapside was born. Le Poulbot has come close in its standards to Le Gavroche and has certainly brought a new dimension to gastronomy in the City for which many people are very appreciative. They have also entered the world of provincial restaurants with their Waterside Inn at Bray-on-Thames, but it is above all for Le Gavroche that they will be remembered.

The two brothers have an unusual relationship with their kitchen staff but it is one that works very well. At regular intervals they turn up in a grey suit which they quickly exchange for a white coat then go into the kitchen to show the staff exactly how they wish something to be cooked. The fact that they are undoubtedly two of the finest chefs in Britain keeps their staff alert and enthusiastic and ensures that standards are maintained. It is also interesting to note that, in the kitchen, the brothers are always called just 'chef' whereas the other staff naturally call them 'M. Roux'.

As Albert Roux is a businessman and his brother an idealist, the guiding principles behind the restaurants are well-balanced and sound; the staff is never required to cook or serve more than one meal per day and fresh ingredients are selected daily from the markets by an experienced buyer who works for them. The result of all this is that the Roux brothers have made a significant contribution to gastronomy in Britain.

London has a number of very fine hotel restaurants apart from the Connaught, but only one of the hotels that have opened since the war has a

3. (a) Thornbury Castle

(b) Kenneth Bell at Thornbury Castle

4. (a) The Connaught
Hotel Grill Room. Tomas
(Sommelier) and Mr.
Simmons (Manager)

(b) Waltons of Walton Street

really exceptional restaurant and that is the Capital in Basil Street. It has certain limitations; for instance the menu does not change often enough to enable *habitués* to go very frequently, but its specialities are so beautifully cooked that the restaurant has well deserved the high esteem in which it is held by many gourmets.

42. David Levin and Richard Shepherd in the kitchens of the Capital Hotel.

The Capital Hotel was opened in May 1971 by David Levin. He had entered the hotel and catering industry at the age of sixteen when he began to work for British Transport Hotels. Then there followed a period of some years during which he went to the Scottish Hotel School and spent a while working in Paris at Les Ambassadeurs and at the Continentale. From Paris he went on to study the hotel industry in Spain before returning to B.T.H. and being taken under the wing of that group's famous hotels manager, Etienne Vacher. The significance of serving under Vacher was that he was a man who regarded the restaurant side of his hotels as being of paramount importance and Levin felt very much in sympathy with this. When he was appointed acting manager of the Great Western Hotel at

Paddington, he made a point of talking to the chef every day and of discussing with him all the dinner parties held in the hotel. It was for this reason that Vacher picked him to go on a sort of culinary crusade to Scotland where he had never been entirely happy about the standard of the restaurant at B.T.H.'s hotel at Kyle of Lochalsh. He appointed Levin as manager there in 1964 and invited him to select a suitable chef from the group. Levin asked the sauce chef at the Caledonian Hotel in Edinburgh to go to Lochalsh as head chef and it was not long before the two of them, working in harmony, had given the hotel a fine reputation for its food.

With all this experience behind him, it is surprising that Levin did not at first contemplate having a restaurant at the Capital. Indeed, the decision was only finally made when he realized that the Government grant of £1,000 per room for new hotels was only available to places having their own restaurant. But having once decided to have a restaurant, Levin was determined that it should be a good one.

Some months before the hotel opened, a chef called Richard Shepherd approached him and asked whether there might be a post available for him in the new hotel. He had started his culinary career at the Cottage-in-the-Woods Hotel at Malvern under Michael Ross and had progressed, via the Savoy and Simpson's, to La Réserve at Beaulieu in the South of France. There he served as *commis tournant* – the man who has to stand in for the vegetable chef, the sauce chef and others on their nights off. He was thus a very experienced chef and, as there were still a few months to go before the opening of the Capital, Levin arranged with his friend Pierre Glaize that he should spend the time working in the kitchen of La Bonne Etape at Chateau Arneau in the Bas-Alpes of which Glaize is the *patron*. He chose this restaurant because it was his favourite place in the whole of France and it was his ambition to create a comparable restaurant in London.

Shepherd and Glaize worked together very successfully and the Frenchman found the Englishman a model pupil. When the hotel finally opened, Glaize came over to England and spent a while in the kitchens at the Capital, helping Shepherd to settle in. The menu they offered was quite small but every item was lovingly prepared. There were three soups, about five first courses including *Filets de Maquereau au vin Blanc* and a *mousseline* of scallops with a cream sauce containing sea urchin, and up to ten main courses of which the great masterpiece was *Loup Capital* – sea bass flavoured with fennel. Other specialities included *darne de saumon sous cloche,** that is salmon poached in fish bouillon and white wine then served with a *beurre*

* When in season!

Nantais – a buttery sauce containing white wine, cream, and shallots, charcoal-grilled lobster with saffron butter and *carré d'agneau aux herbes de Provence*.

To accompany these dishes Levin built up a wine list that offered a choice of twenty-three clarets of which nineteen were Château-bottled and included first and second growths of the better years of the 1950s, ten white burgundies, fourteen red burgundies, and more than a dozen Hocks and Loire wines. As a lover of port, he has made sure that some outstanding vintages are always available.

The only cloud on the horizon in the early days of the Capital was that no one came to eat there! Day after day only half a dozen covers would be served at lunch and fewer still at dinner, but morale remained high and standards too. There was no advertising of any sort and so it was not until Quentin Crewe happened to go there and followed his visit by writing a very enthusiastic article that people really heard of it. The restaurant, which is limited to thirty-five covers at lunch and at dinner has been fully booked every day ever since then, but standards have not suffered at all. The kitchen staff has increased from two to eight and, as there is a shift system, no one is ever asked to cook both lunch and dinner on the same day. Nor is there ever a desperate rush, Levin being very firm about limiting the total number of covers to seventy per day so that the kitchen can never be over-stretched.

The 1960s is an exciting period in the story of good restaurants outside London and these began to open in such large numbers after 1965 that it is not at all easy to assess which proprietors have played the most significant part in the development of provincial gastronomy. When I say 'such large numbers' it is of course only in comparison with the 1950s. In that decade only two or three exceptionally good restaurants opened outside London whereas in the 1960s and early 1970s the number has been more like twenty-five.

One *restaurateur* who has an undisputed place in any list of leading figures of the 1960s is Kenneth Bell. He comes from a family that was not particularly interested in food and his own interest in the subject dates from his years in the Royal Artillery when he served in the Middle East, France and Italy. After leaving the Army in 1948 he received a further education grant which enabled him to go to the Ecole Hotelière at Lausanne. There he spent five months on each of three courses in different aspects of hotel management and of cooking and came out as top graduate of his year, a feat very rarely achieved by a non-Swiss. Thereafter, he spent a while as manager of the Château de Montreuil near Boulogne and at various hotels in England before finally deciding that he really wanted to be a *restaurateur*.

He began his search for a suitable place in 1959 and after rejecting numerous possibilities came across a café with a club licence in Oxford, called the Elizabeth.

Having once acquired the restaurant, Bell decided to do all the cooking himself and he was extremely fortunate in finding a certain Antonio Lopez whom he appointed as head waiter. Lopez was an experienced waiter but had not been able to find a suitable job in England after moving here from Spain and for a while had wasted his talents serving in a very humble capacity at Brown's Hotel in London. As a large proportion of the staff were Spanish, Bell was influenced to make his cooking Mediterranean in style rather than classically French. This school of cuisine is stronger and more spicy and is a little easier to prepare than classical French cooking.

Bell was fortunate in picking Oxford as his starting-point because his clientele of dons, better-off undergraduates, doctors, and solicitors was probably far more ready to accept his exotic cooking than people in almost any other provincial city. He says he was very much influenced by George Perry-Smith, whose restaurant at Bath he had visited on numerous occasions, and also by Patrick Gibbings of the Monkey Island Hotel at Bray. His formula worked well in Oxford and soon the Elizabeth, once popular for its meat and two veg, became renowned for *piperade*, prawns in *aioli*, *taramasalata*, *coq au vin*, *moussaka*, and *creme brulée*. The only problem was the wine.

Bell had acquired with the restaurant a curious mixture of wines. There were crates of Cyprus sherry and plenty of Spanish *vin ordinaire* as well as a plentiful supply of exquisite vintages from the 1930s. The explanation for this curious phenomenon, he later found out, was that the previous proprietor of the Elizabeth had lived in Harpenden and regularly passed the Victoria Wine Company in St. Albans on her way in to Oxford. This wine shop had never bothered to increase the prices of its older wines which, by the late 1950s, had come to be among the cheapest available and so, naturally, she had bought them in large quantities for her restaurant.

Gradually, Bell made his cellar far better balanced and his wine education was furthered by Ted Hale of Harveys who was an excellent teacher in this most complex subject. But the problem remained: people would come into the restaurant and salivate over the sight of racks of tempting-looking bottles round the walls, only to be told that they had to join the Elizabeth Club forty-eight hours in advance if they wished to be served with wine.

One of the key reasons for the difficulty in obtaining a licence was that the restaurant only had one loo. Bell eventually overcame this by finding a number of customers who readily volunteered to stand up in court and declare that they had never been distressed or inconvenienced in any way by the fact that there was just the one solitary pedestal. The licence was granted in 1961.

43. Kenneth Bell in the kitchen
at Thornbury Castle.

Bell feels that it took about three years before the Elizabeth was really good and thereafter he continued to run it very happily for a further two or three years. Then, by about 1965, he began to feel its limitations. It was extremely small, it had very little storage space and no proper cellar and so he began to think of moving on. During his search for a suitable restaurant in 1959 he had come across a fine 16th century castle at Thornbury near

Bristol which had once been the home of Mary Tudor. He had been tempted by it but had not felt confident enough to take it on as his first independent venture. By 1966 he was far more certain of his own abilities and also Thornbury had become a more suitable location for a restaurant because of its proximity to the newly-constructed motorway. As it was still available, he bought Thornbury Castle in 1966 and sold the Elizabeth to his head waiter, Antonio Lopez, who maintains a very high standard there still.

At Thornbury, Bell's approach was slightly different: he explained in his brochure that his aim was to run the sort of country restaurant that one might find in France, where one could get a good meal without being pretentious. To this end he included on the menu many classical and *bourgeois* French dishes such as *moules à l'escargot, quenelles de saumon à la crême, mousseline* of salmon in pastry and chicken or pheasant with apple, cream and calvados, without abandoning the Mediterranean dishes. He also attempted to offer a five-course fixed-price menu with a choice of at least two dishes for each course. To begin with, his customers could have a soup or a *pâté* then go on to a *quiche* or fish course, a main course of meat, game or poultry, cheese, and a pudding. This idea did not work out, as his customers felt that they were being told what to choose and resented this. Another hazard was that all the diners, having paid a fixed price for their five courses, insisted on gobbling up every morsel that was set before them and then complained bitterly that they felt uncomfortably full!

The food guides quickly gave Thornbury Castle the highest possible rating, placing it on a par with the Savoy Grill and Gleneagles. The result of this was that people would arrive at the Castle and say to Bell 'We've come to test you out'. He hated the 'Temple of Gastronomy' image and merely wanted people to enjoy themselves. He also wanted people to expand their gastronomic horizons when they came to his restaurant by being a little more adventurous than usual. He used to make a point of encouraging diners to try his French dishes instead of ordering simple grills but found that they were not easily persuaded and so now, on an average evening, more than half the customers order grills.

One way in which Bell is, to the best of my knowledge, unique among British *restaurateurs* is that he is also a *vigneron*. Vines grow all round the castle area and come close to the ancient walls. The wine is very drinkable and is offered at the Castle at a modest price. But for those who do not wish to drink this most unusual house wine, there is a very fine cellar.

Returning to the early 1960s, the Miners' Arms at Priddy, which had come to fame in the late 1950s as a result of the efforts of Colonel House, developed still further after being taken over by Mr. and Mrs. Paul Leyton in 1961. Leyton had devoted his life to science and had spent many years helping to build rockets for the Government. Then he moved into industry and was appointed Director of Engineering for Black and Decker. A time came, however, when he felt he wanted to work for himself, so he decided that he would find a suitable pub and run it together with his wife. They spent some time looking at various possible places but none of them ever seemed entirely suitable. Finally, they heard that the Miners' Arms was up for sale and, though they had not intended to run a restaurant, they decided to take it on.

The first changes that they brought in were not so much gastronomic ones as sensible steps to bring the restaurant into line with most other civilized places. They started to offer their diners an aperitif before their meal and brandy and liqueurs afterwards and when they had settled in for long enough to be sure that everything was running well, they began to take a close look at the cooking. The worst defect in the menu they had inherited lay in the basic white sauce which was used for everything; for meat dishes a little stock was added, for fish dishes a little anchovy essence, but otherwise it was always the same. Leyton restructured the menu to ensure that every dish had its own individually-made sauce and began to introduce new specialities from time to time, most of which can never be found at any other restaurant in Britain.

Like most people, Leyton knew that the ordinary snails found in gardens in this country can be poisonous, but he also realized that, if the snails were starved for a period, any poisonous fungus they might have eaten would be digested and so the snails would become harmless. This sounds cruel but, in fact, it is not, since a snail can survive for periods of a year or more without either food or water and the starvation period for restaurant purposes is no more than a week. And so Mendip snails are served regularly at the Miners' Arms with a sauce made of local butter, cream, and herbs. Another speciality introduced by Leyton is the Priddy Oggy. This looks rather like a Cornish pasty but is quite different: the pastry is given a delicious cheesy flavour and inside is placed a piece of fillet of pork wrapped round with some smoked pork. The meat is smoked on the premises and Leyton always keeps some loins of pork and calves' tongues up in his drawing-room chimney for use in the restaurant. Apart from being used in the oggy, the smoked pork is served very thinly sliced as a first course and is rather similar to Parma ham. The smoked calves' tongues are used in another first course called a Priddy Oyster. This dish consists of a piece of

44. Mr. and Mrs. Paul Leyton at the Miners' Arms, Priddy.

forcemeat made of the tongues, wrapped round with a slice of calf's sweet-bread and fried in its own juices in a dry frying-pan.

In recent years Leyton has become so distressed by the very sharp rise in wine prices that he has used his scientific knowledge to enable his customers to drink well at modest prices. In close consultation with Averys of Bristol he has chosen five house-wines which he buys in one-gallon glass jars. They comprise a white Bordeaux, a claret, a *Rosé* from Beaujolais, a white burgundy, and a red burgundy. To these jars he connects a system of taps and tubes and cylinders which automatically pump carbon dioxide into the jars at slightly less than atmospheric pressure as the wine is drawn out. In this way the wine remains in almost perfect condition for up to two weeks.

Leyton has found that German wines do not stand up to this treatment very well and so he always has a house Hock available by the bottle. He has also always had an English wine available by the bottle but now that supplies of the Beaulieu Abbey *Rosé* have come to an end, he is not certain that this tradition can continue.

Altogether the Miners' Arms is a most original and fascinating place.

Many of the comments made in this book will doubtless arouse vehement criticism and denials from readers but I now offer an exception to the rule when I say that Malcolm Reid and Colin Long of the Box Tree Cottage at Ilkley, Yorkshire, are the two most enthusiastic *restaurateurs* in Britain. It is so blatantly true to anyone who has met them that there can be no denial! The result of all this enthusiasm is that the Box Tree Cottage has been one of the finest provincial restaurants in Britain ever since it opened. 'We appreciate the arts,' they say, 'but to sit down and have a meal and lovely wine is the greatest thing in life. Our life, our whole being is centred round going to great restaurants.'

Reid and Long both began life in the same business; they were salesmen for men's clothes, but both of them shared a profound enthusiasm for gastronomy. They made a point of meeting at regular intervals to try out restaurants in Yorkshire and the surrounding area and, when they had

45. Malcolm Reid and Colin Long.

saved up a little money, even ventured south as far as the Savoy Grill. After a while they began to wonder if they would be able to reproduce some of the dishes they had enjoyed, and experiments in their own kitchens revealed that they obviously did have a certain amount of natural ability. Gradually the idea dawned on them that they ought to open a restaurant. Neither of them had had any experience of catering except that Reid's mother had cooked for members of the Lithuanian aristocracy and his father had at one time run a small buffet in Leeds. Nevertheless, in 1962, they acquired a small defunct tea-shop in Ilkley called the Box Tree Cottage and, without taking on any staff, began to serve afternoon tea. When they found that this was going reasonably well, they decided to be braver and so opened for lunch. When that too proved a success, they began to take on more staff and to serve dinners instead of lunches.

At the end of a year their efforts were rewarded when they received a star in the *Egon Ronay Guide*. By the following year they had jumped to three stars and while countless other restaurants have come and gone, theirs has retained its top-class rating ever since. How has this been achieved? The answer is by dedication. Although there is a total kitchen staff of eight including the two proprietors (and they never leave the kitchen while the restaurant is open) Reid and Long normally get to work every day at about 9.30 a.m. and often do not get back to their home in Leeds until 2 a.m. the next morning. They claim that they are still just as nervous every night as they were on the opening night and they are both adamant in saying that even after all this time, they find food every bit as fascinating as when they first began.

In order to recharge their batteries and to keep in perfect gastronomic trim they make a point of closing their restaurant from time to time so that they can go and explore other exciting restaurants in France. They often make use of the day on which the restaurant is closed each week to fly off to France for a good dinner. Both the partners adore drinking wine and they have built up what is almost certainly the finest cellar outside London, the only possible rival being the Bell at Aston Clinton. The Box Tree wine list offers a choice of some 300 vintages and for anyone who takes the trouble to telephone in advance and discuss their favourite wines, there is a further reserve of about 100 items. This final hundred is really the proprietors' personal cellar but they are usually willing to part with an odd bottle if they believe that the customer is a true enthusiast.

The restaurant offers a four-course set menu (or five courses if one has cheese as well as a pudding) with a choice of three or four items at each course. They do not have specialities as they change the menu regularly and only serve what they really enjoy cooking. However, just to give some indication of the sort of items one might expect to find, I will reproduce here the menu of a dinner I enjoyed there a few months ago:

Escargots de Bourgogne
Fresh Tomato and Orange Soup
Fillet of Lamb in a cream and Vermouth sauce with morels
Haricots verts
White Stilton
Raspberry Vacherin

Being in a remote corner of Yorkshire has not made it easy for the Box Tree to obtain really good fresh supplies. It took the proprietors a long time to get local suppliers to obtain such items as *mange-touts* for them and their beef is sent over 400 miles from northern Scotland. Their lobsters also come from Scotland, and their oysters from Cornwall. Whenever either of them is in London for any reason, he always fills his car to capacity with all sorts of supplies that are impossible to obtain in Yorkshire.

As Reid and Long are amateurs they have found it best to take on in-experienced kitchen staff and train them in their own ways. Their staff are just as enthusiastic as they are and most of them stay on for years. They all thought that they had reached the high-spot of their career in 1971 when the Box Tree was given the Restaurant of the Year award but little did they know that further honours were in store for them.

In 1972 they acquired a splendid Jacobean mansion called Kildwick Hall, only about ten minutes' drive from Ilkley. There they decided to open a second restaurant, using staff that had been entirely trained by them. The result of this was that at the end of its first year of operation, Kildwick Hall was given the Restaurant of the Year award for 1973 and promises to be as great a restaurant as the Box Tree itself.

All the restaurants we have looked at in this chapter so far, with the exception of the Connaught Hotel, have been independent of any group. It is always far harder for a restaurant that is part of a large chain or group to excel since the management usually lacks the vital personal touch which inspires the staff and especially the chef. It is, therefore, in some ways, an even greater achievement on the part of British Transport Hotels to have created a restaurant of exceptional merit than it would have been on the part of an individual proprietor. British Transport Hotels have always offered a standard of cooking that was well above average and they have always been famed for their wine lists but, since the early 1960s, one restaur-ant in the group has stood out as being specially good: the French Restaur-ant at the Midland Hotel in Manchester.

The reason for the excellence of this particular restaurant lies in the fact that B.T.H. has had a long tradition of French chefs in its top hotels and the central management of the group has made a point of recruiting some of the finest chefs in France. In 1962 they recruited a man of outstanding ability and appointed him chef at the French Restaurant.

Gilbert Lèfevre was only thirty-one years old when he came to the Midland Hotel but he had had plenty of experience. He had begun his culinary life in the South of France, where he worked at the Relais de la

46. The French Restaurant at the Midland Hotel, Manchester.

Méditerranée in Nice. Later he moved to the Hotel Negresco, also in Nice, and then more recently to the Hotel Plaza Athénée in Paris. At the Midland he has offered the citizens of Manchester, a city which is still, sadly, something of a gastronomic wilderness, dishes of a standard that cannot be found for many miles around. There is not space to mention all his specialities, but here are just a few of them; for the rest, the menu offers classical French dishes almost all of which are very competently cooked:

Potage du Var: a fish bouillon with white wine, saffron, egg yolks, and cream. It is served with garlic *croûtons.*

Côte de Bœuf Vigneronne: Beef cooked in a burgundy sauce and served with grapes and bone marrow.

Soufflé d'Homard Montaigne: Diced lobster meat flamed in brandy with shallots and butter then placed in the bottom of a *soufflé* mould. A Gruyére *soufflé* forms the top layer. It is served with *sauce nantua.*

47. Gilbert Lefèvre.

It must have seemed to people that, with the passing of men like John Fothergill and Barry Neame, the day of the larger-than-life *patron*, whose customers were always slightly overawed, was over, but this is not so. The tradition is carried on to this day by one of Britain's largest *restauteururs*, Patrick Stevenson who owns a restaurant called the Horn of Plenty at Gulworthy in Devon.

Like so many of our greatest *restaurateurs*, Stevenson and his wife are amateurs. He devoted many years of his life to working for the Southern Railway before giving this up to become an opera singer, while she was a violinist. However, they both share an enormous enthusiasm for good food and this prompted Sonia Stevenson to begin to cook when they were married. She has never had any proper cookery lessons but she is one of those rare people who, with the help of sound instincts, is able to follow a recipe from

48. Mr. and Mrs. Patrick Stevenson
at the Horn of Plenty, Gulworthy.

a book and create from it a culinary masterpiece. The books she has been
particularly impressed by are the works of Elizabeth David and Philip
Harben as well as Samuel Chamberlain's *Bouquet de France*. She has also
received a certain amount of helpful advice from chefs at restaurants she
has visited, both in England and in France, and all this has made her a
truly remarkable cook.

The menu at the Horn of Plenty is very seasonal and one reason for this
is that the Stevensons grow a large proportion of the vegetables and fruit
themselves. The cooking is, generally speaking, a mixture of English and
French provincial dishes and in the evening a French regional menu

complete with wines of that particular area is offered at a fixed price as an alternative to the *à la carte* menu. Mrs. Stevenson also has a list of dishes which are available to those ordering a few days in advance for parties of about ten people and these include a whole ham cooked *en croûte* with truffles, whole turkey stuffed with fresh herbs from the Stevensons' garden and lobster *Charentaise* – that is lobster with a cream, vermouth, and mustard sauce.

I have had so many memorable dishes at the Horn of Plenty that it is difficult to know which ones were the best, but I must mention the duck *pâté* which is served inside a boned duck so that there is some fresh roasted duck-meat surrounding each slice, the *noisettes d'agneau en croûte* with chopped mushrooms and the pigeon with juniper berries.

Finally, we must come back to Robert Carrier who, as I mentioned, has now become a leading provincial *restaurateur* without neglecting his London interests. In common with a great many Londoners, Carrier has always enjoyed spending some time in the country at week-ends but when he had a country house he found that he always had a guilty conscience when he was there; he felt he ought to be working. The result was that he very rarely visited his country home and therefore eventually sold it but, after doing so, realized that he missed it. He then thought that if he could buy a fine country mansion and create a restaurant there he would both be able to enjoy spending far more time in the country and would also be able to avoid that guilty feeling that worried him so much, since it would be his business as well as his home. He spent some time scanning the advertisements in *Country Life* and other magazines but no obviously suitable house came up. Finally, while he was on holiday in St. Tropez in 1971 some friends contacted him and said they had found just the right place for him. He cut short his holiday and found on his return that his friends had reserved a beautiful house in Suffolk called Hintlesham Hall. The origins of the Hall go back to the time of Henry VIII but its character is certainly that of the Queen Anne period.

Carrier lost little time in making up his mind to buy the house and in setting to work on designs for a dream kitchen that would serve the restaurant. He also undertook a major renovation programme to restore the Hall to its former glory, the most tricky part of which was the restoration of the moulded ceiling in the Caroline Room. Although work did not start on all this until January 1972 and his advisors told him that the whole operation would take more than a year to complete, Carrier was determined to open the Hall in July so that the musical festival, which had been held there

49. Hintlesham Hall.

annually for more than twenty years under the previous owner, Antony Scott Stokes, would not have to be suspended. With the full force of Carrier's enthusiastic encouragement behind it, the work was miraculously completed in time and the festival with its concerts, lectures, banquets, and grand ball was an even greater success than usual.

The opening night of the festival filled the Hall to capacity and Carrier was very pleased to see that all the gloomy predictions of his friends who had said that he would never find enough custom to support such a special restaurant in Suffolk had proved to be wrong. But they were not wrong and to his dismay, Carrier found himself with an almost empty restaurant soon after the festival had ended. For a while he was seriously worried but then gradually word went round the district about how wonderful both the setting and the food and wine were at the Hall and this tempted the residents of that part of Suffolk to begin making gastronomic pilgrimages to the restaurant. More and more people also began to visit it from further afield, so that by Christmas 1972 it was usually full and this pressure has been maintained ever since. An average of 500 people are now fed there every week.

The cooking is, of course, very much the same as at the Islington restaurant and the menu is set out in the same way, that is with a four-course fixed price *table d'hôte*. The specialities include *brandade* of Colchester smoked mackerel, duckling with *Sauerkraut*, partridge with grapes and Mr. Carrier's chocolate fancy as well as some of the luscious *pâtés*, *terrines*, and *quiches* which made the London restaurant famous.

Hintlesham is already more than just a restaurant – it is an institution. Where else can diners drink their apéritives in the Long Gallery or Justices' Room and then move in to the Red Room or China Room for dinner before finally retiring to the Great Saloon for their brandy, coffee, and cigars? Or what other restaurant has an annual festival of arts and music as well as a gourmet dining club? Truly, Carrier, with his Islington restaurant and Hintlesham Hall, his numerous cookery books and kitchen equipment shops has done more for gastronomy in Britain than any other *restaurateur* since George Perry-Smith.

*   *   *

The only restaurant of outstanding merit to have opened in London since the Capital Hotel is Walton's of Walton Street and its success is perhaps understandable when one learns that its young proprietor, Malcolm

Livingstone, comes from Ilkley in Yorkshire. There, from an early age, he came under the influence of Malcolm Reid and Colin Long at the Box Tree Cottage and eventually, at about the time he was leaving school, they made him their head waiter. Some months later, in order to gain more experience, he went to work in a small hotel in Normandy and on to one in Germany before returning to England to take a four-year course in hotel management at Leeds. After that, he came to work for Robert Carrier at Islington and impressed his employer sufficiently to be invited to be the first manager of Hintlesham Hall. It was while he was there that two friends approached him and offered to give him some financial backing if he opened a restaurant of his own. That was how Walton's came to be born in November 1973.

Livingstone was fortunate in numbering among his friends Mike Smith, a former Yorkshire *restaurateur* turned designer, who transformed what had been Chez Luba's Russian restaurant into the wonderland of pastel shades that now is Walton's. He was also extremely fortunate in being able to secure the services of Ernst Stark as his head chef. Livingstone, Stark, and Mike Smith jointly created the rather unusual and delicious menus offered at the restaurant and they have always made a point of including one or two 18th century English dishes as Mike Smith is an expert on the subject.

There is a two-course and a three-course *table d'hôte* menu at lunch and a four-course one at dinner with a reasonable choice of dishes at each course (though the total number of dishes offered is small enough to ensure that everything can be properly prepared). The menu does not reflect any particular school of cooking except that one might say that in creating so many original dishes, Livingstone and his colleagues have carried on where Ray Parkes left off. Here are some examples of their dishes:

> *Pâté* of frogs' legs
> Terrine of sweet herbs in a crust
> Courgette and fennel soup
> Mussel cream pie (a pastry shell with a filling of
> eggs, cream and mussels)

> Arabic lamb stew
> *Ragoût* of roe deer
> *Brochette* of fillets of sole with king prawns, *sauce Choron*

Among the 18th century English dishes they have offered are Jole of salmon with ginger (that is salmon cooked in a puff pastry case with raisins and stem ginger and served with a rich egg sauce) and sole cooked with orange, capers, and anchovy. Naturally, they also offer a number of more conventional dishes for the menus are well planned to give a balance of rich as well as simple foods.

The only slightly disappointing feature of the menu is the puddings; these are all cold and for the most part are good but not exceptional. However, even here, an effort has been made to offer something a little out of the ordinary such as home-made mango ice-cream or old English chocolate pye.* There is normally a savoury available as well.

The cellar is a very fine one, especially considering that it was only assembled in the latter half of 1973. Among more than 200 wines offered there are twenty-eight *Château*-bottled clarets including several from the 1940s and 1950s and the selection of Burgundies, Rhône wines, Hocks, and Moselles is splendid too. Best of all, Mr. Livingstone has found in Jacques Sallé an outstanding *sommelier*. Sallé is utterly dedicated to his art and although he was only twenty-seven at the time the restaurant opened, his knowledge and experience are remarkable. With such a large selection of wines, the problem of always having bottles available at the correct serving temperature is a considerable one. The wine dispensary has been well organized and can usually cope but, when Mr. Livingstone knows that a great wine-lover is coming to the restaurant, he usually contacts him so that the wine can be ordered in advance if desired. In this way it is possible to avoid keeping the rarer vintages in the dispensary where they might, if unsold, quite soon deteriorate.

There can be no doubt that the advent of Malcolm Livingstone and Walton's has been very good for the gastronomic world of London for they appeared at a time when the prospect of there ever being any more really good new restaurants had begun to seem bleak.

* '*Pye*' is the correct spelling!

Chapter 6

THE RISE OF GASTRONOMY IN SCOTLAND

SCOTLAND produces some of the finest raw materials for the table that can be found anywhere and it is with good reason that its Aberdeen-Angus beef, its venison, grouse, and salmon are known throughout the world. It is therefore only logical that Scotland should be important gastronomically but, in fact, outstandingly good restaurants did not exist there at all until the twenties and, even now, they are not particularly numerous. One must conclude that the reason for this is that the Puritan ethos has lingered on north of the border even longer than in England and has denied Scotsmen the privilege of being brought up to think about and really enjoy their food. Happily, the signs are that this is beginning to change and I believe that the standard of Scottish restaurants will rise over the next few years. In the meantime, let us take a look at some of the pioneers of good food in Scotland.

I hope that it will not come as too unpleasant a shock to my Scottish friends to learn that the creator of the first good restaurants in Scotland was an Englishman. His name was Arthur Towle and you may remember that I mentioned him and his father, Sir William Towle, when I was discussing the early days of English provincial restaurants.

Sir William Towle was the creator of the great railway hotels that began to appear in various parts of England in the latter part of the 19th century and, throughout his life, was deeply interested in improving travelling amenities. He passed this interest on to his son Arthur, who, after leaving Marlborough travelled extensively in Europe and America to study the latest developments in the hotel and restaurant world. As a result both of his upbringing and of his travels, he became seriously interested in good food and so, when he began to reach the top of the hierarchy in the Midland Railway Company, he used his influence to raise the standard of cuisine in the company's hotels.

In 1923, the Caledonian Railway Company became part of the London, Midland and Scottish Railway Company and so Towle was able to begin to exert his influence on the hotels that had belonged to the Caledonian group. This influence was first felt at the Gleneagles Hotel. The Caledonian Railway had begun construction work there in 1914 and by 1923 it was nearing completion. Towle busied himself immediately with all the furnishing and equipping of the new hotel.

Gleneagles opened in June 1924 and its Restaurant Fleuri was the first French restaurant in Scotland. The railway archives describe it as, 'A French restaurant *par excellence*. The soft, pastel greys of the walls are broken up with Parma violets and enormous suspended Louis XVI baskets of brilliant blossoms. . . . The cooking is characterized by wonderful delicacy and variety.'

The Restaurant Fleuri no longer exists and the hotel's restaurant is now called the Glendevon Room. However, a worthy successor to the Fleuri is the Restaurant du Soleil which still functions at the hotel during the high season. In August some particularly good French dishes are served such as *paupiettes de sole Gleneagles* – stuffed fillets of sole with diced lobster, shrimps, and mushrooms in a white wine and lobster sauce – and *suprême de volaille aux morilles*.

Towle's second French restaurant in Scotland opened only three years after the first. It was the Malmaison at the Central Hotel in Glasgow, so named because the décor was copied from the Chateau de Malmaison, the

50. The Malmaison Restaurant, Central Hotel, Glasgow in 1927.

palace of the Empress Josephine, wife of Napoleon. When he felt satisfied that all was going well at the Malmaison, Towle turned his attention to the Caledonian Hotel in Edinburgh. He engaged a French chef and although no separate French restaurant was established there, the hotel soon began to offer some examples of *haute cuisine* in the Degrees Rooms. It was only in 1953, five years after Towle's death, that the present French restaurant at the Caledonian, the Pompadour, was opened.

Towle established certain important policies in Scotland in the early days which British Transport Hotels still adhere to. First, all the French restaurants had to have a French chef. Actually, the present chef at the Pompadour is a French-trained Englishman but he is entirely worthy of B.T.H.'s tradition. Secondly, all hotel managers and chefs were instructed to make a study of the best fresh ingredients available in the locality of their hotel and to bear this in mind when drawing up their menus. He was always anxious that each restaurant should be autonomous. Only in the matter of wine buying were individual managers not given their freedom. This has always been done centrally for the whole group and it has been done extremely well.

For a while, the railway hotels were the only outposts of gastronomy in Scotland but then a very important figure came on the scenes in the person of William Heptinstall. In 1929 he was brave enough to take the lease of a hotel in the Highlands several miles from the nearest railway station and there he practised his culinary art so successfully that by 1945 André Simon expressed the opinion that there was no better food to be found in Britain than at Heptinstall's hotel at Fortingall.

Heptinstall was born at Pontefract in 1890 and was the son of a confectioner. After learning his father's art, he went on to work as a chef at various hotels, including the Charing Cross Hotel in London and the Adelphi in Liverpool. He also spent some time as chef at Lord's Cricket Ground. His great enthusiasm soon made him want to travel abroad so that he could see at first hand how foreign dishes were prepared in their native countries and he visited Austria, Hungary, Czechoslovakia, Italy, France, and, later, America. During these travels he worked in such places as the Carlton Hotel in Budapest and the Continentale in Paris and this was how he came to be such a perfectionist, all through his life he prepared dishes in the authentic way and never used short-cuts or improvised methods which might have lowered his standards.

After returning to England, he went back into the family confectionery business but soon found that, much as he liked his brother, he was not the

51. William Heptinstall at his famous cold table.

52. Fortingall Hotel.

ideal business partner. He decided to look out for a hotel of his own and found it at Fortingall.

Even today, traffic is very light in the Highlands but in the 1920s cars were very few and far between, so it must have taken enormous courage to set up in a spot that was so far from a main railway line. All those who wished to come to his hotel could only get within about eight miles by rail and even that meant taking an infrequent service along a branch line. Nevertheless, he was determined to succeed and although business was decidedly slack at first, he never compromised his standards nor did he hesitate to include in his menus dishes that most of his visitors had never heard of, let alone tasted, before coming to Fortingall. The result was that, before very long, word began to go round that a visit to his hotel could be a special experience and, although the Scots were certainly not anything like as gastronomically minded then as they are today, business began to pick up considerably. It is true that Heptinstall did have a certain advantage in the situation of his hotel in spite of its distance from the railway. It was set in some of the most beautiful countryside in Scotland and the churchyard just near the hotel is said to contain the oldest living thing in the British Isles, a three thousand year old yew tree. Furthermore, the district offered a number of attractions to lovers of sporting life. One admirer has this to say about it: 'I went first to Fortingall, not because of the fishing which is first-rate, nor because of the deer-stalking, though there were so many stags that I should not have been surprised to find one in the lounge – nor to shoot grouse, of which the supply both on the table and out of doors was to a Sassenach little short of miraculous . . . but to explore Glen Lyon and use it as a centre for a general tour of the Highlands'. These attractions helped the business until the reputation for outstanding cuisine made the hotel less dependent on what might be called Glen Lyon's fringe benefits.

Many Frenchmen use the phrase '*Temple de la gastronomie*' to describe an outstanding restaurant off the beaten track, in other words somewhere that is so good that it is worthwhile putting up with a certain amount of inconvenience to be able to enjoy its cuisine and cellar. This phrase is particularly apt for Fortingall since Heptinstall was something of a disciplinarian and his guests had to obey his rules. To many people the restrictions and discomforts were a penance they gladly paid to enjoy the rest: the bar only opened for a very short time before meals and closed as soon as the gong sounded and guests were expected to be punctual for meals. Another excellent rule was that smoking was not allowed in the dining-room at any time. Nor were the surroundings in which all this superb food and wine were consumed sumptuous, the dining-room was cold and austere and more than one guest described the lounge as 'morgue-like'. Despite all this, very few guests ever went away disappointed and most were profoundly impressed.

Fortingall menus were beautifully balanced and offered an astonishing mixture of *haute cuisine* and *bourgeois* dishes from all over Europe. At lunch-time there was a limited choice but at dinner the guests were obliged to take what was offered or do without. It was only in this way that 'Hep' as he was known, was able to offer such good food at such moderate prices, for no effort or ingredients ever need be wasted. Here are two typical Fortingall dinner menus:

Chachouka	*Gnocchi alla Toscana*
Consommé aux Oeufs Filés	*Consommé Nature*
Caneton Braisé a l'orange	*Truite Grenobloise*
Glace au Four	*Poulet Braisé Brésilien*
Champignons à ma façon	*Flan à ma façon*

Lunches, as I said, offered a limited choice and here is a typical luncheon menu:

Minestrone
Crème Carmen
Grilled Salmon *sauce Remoulade*
Risotto di Scampi
Perdreaux aux choux
Cold: Grouse pie
Venison
Ham
Tongue

Poires Cardinal
Bandeau Meringue aux Abricots
Banana Ice Cream

Cheese Board

Other favourite first courses included local smoked salmon, *beignets au fromage* and several kinds of *quiche*. 'Hep' was also famed for his succulent *crêpes* and his splendid cellar could match any menu perfectly. However his greatest speciality of all was the cold table. Cold table was only offered once a week at the hotel and that was as a prelude to Sunday lunch. It was easy to see who were the *habitués* and who were not because the former wisely helped themselves in moderation knowing that they had four delicious courses to follow, whereas the latter piled their plates as if they were stocking up for a week. On an average Sunday no less than forty dishes would be offered of which at least half had to be prepared before breakfast.

Hep deplored the usual sort of *hors-d'œuvres* consisting of 'beetroot, radishes, and sliced tomato to give colour accompanied by a few dried-up sardines and baked beans served fresh from the tin'. His philosophy was this:

'Just as a good or bad start may win or lose the race, so may *hors-d'œuvres* make or mar a meal. Unless they are dainty, little, and tasty, they will dull the keen edge of your appetite.' He saw to it that none of his Sunday lunchers ever had their edges dulled.

After the war, Fortingall Hotel rightly had the reputation of being one of the very few places left in which the best traditional methods were still used; indeed, it was just about the only place left with a direct link, in the person of Hep, with the Edwardian heyday of *haute cuisine*. This, of course, made many enthusiastic young men entering the catering trade anxious to find employment there. It was partly because Hep had done so much to train a new generation of highly competent and enthusiastic chefs and because he devoted much time to such things as judging the Scottish Salon Culinaire that, in 1964, he was made the first honorary member of the *Association Culinaire Français* and was awarded its Gold Medal. This was to mark his retirement after thirty-five years at Fortingall.

Hep died about five years after retiring and of all those upon whom it might be said that his mantle has descended, the most deserving is probably Keith Knight, who is at present *patron* of Houstoun House at Uphall near Edinburgh.

Knight began working at Fortingall in 1956 and, although he was twenty-six years old, he was only earning £3 for a seven-day week with long hours. This did not worry him at all for he had never been happier. His first year was spent in the dining-room where, among other things, he was able to begin building up a knowledge of wine by tasting the drops left in the bottom of decanters when the guests had left. During the winter, when the hotel was very quiet, he spent several weeks taking stock of the cellar, another useful experience. In his second year at the hotel, Knight worked in the kitchen with Heptinstall and it was there that the foundation of his skill was laid; many of the succulent sauces served at Houstoun House today are those that Hep taught him to make at that time.

After leaving Fortingall, Knight worked for a while in a hotel in Perth and then took on a place of his own, the Royal Hotel at Comrie, where he opened for business in November 1961. At this time, virtually all the takings came from the bar, though a total of six dinners were served that winter – to the same family of three, twice! The Knights used the quiet winter period to redecorate the hotel and, with the coming of spring, established a four-course set dinner in the dining-room along the lines laid down at Fortingall. This was done very much against the advice of many of his friends who told him that all people wanted was good, plain, simple, British cooking but Knight knew that if he were to avoid going broke, he would have to establish

53. Mr. and Mrs. Keith Knight.

a reputation quickly. The good, plain, simple cooking was not the way to achieve this. As it turned out, he was quite right and soon his interesting four-course dinners had become quite famous in the district. Business was also helped in the second year by the hotel being featured in the *Good Food Guide* after which its success was assured. The Royal Hotel remains to this day among the best restaurants in Scotland.

In spite of the success of the Royal after its first year, the Knights were not entirely happy there because the winter months were so very quiet. They had the choice of keeping their staff and losing money or losing the staff, and they found it frustrating to have just enough business to prevent them from relaxing, but not enough to enable them to make money. They therefore decided in 1967 to look out for a suitable building of some historical interest that they could convert into a hotel with a first-class restaurant. Knight, who had originally trained as an architect, was well qualified to make this search and he eventually found Houstoun House at Uphall. The property had never been on the market since it was built in 1569 because it had remained in the Shairp family until it was sold to the sitting tenant, Ian Lindsey, the famous Scottish architect, in 1945.

Knight decided that it was just the place for him but, having begun the process of buying it, he found that there were a number of hazards on the horizon. The first of these was the problem of obtaining a licence, for Uphall was in an area where the number of licences permitted was strictly limited.

In order to do something about this, he had to organize a petition to the local council. Finally, after numerous delays and setbacks, the licence was granted on the morning of the day on which the restaurant was due to open.

Another problem centred round the fact that Houstoun House is a scheduled building, a national treasure of Scotland. This meant that all plans for converting it into an hotel and building an extension had to be submitted not only to the county council but also to the Scottish Office and the Historic Buildings Commission. After lengthy negotiations, in which Knight found his architect's training a great help, permission was finally granted. Building operations began in April 1969 and the restaurant opened in December of the same year. Bookings have been very heavy ever since the opening day.

Knight has used the time since the opening of Houstoun House to build up one of the finest cellars in Britain. His wine list, which began by offering a choice of eighty wines, now offers 180 vintages and the cellar is stocked with over 12,000 bottles.

54. Houstoun House from the garden.

Houstoun House has already proved itself to be a great success but Knight, being something of a perfectionist, has not yet fulfilled his ambitions. The cost of setting up Houstoun was so much greater than expected that he has been obliged to run it on slightly more commercial lines than he would have wished. That is to say, he has to serve rather more lunches and dinners than he would like and, worst of all, he has to remain open for 363 days in the year. His dream is, therefore, to move away from Uphall in a few years time and set up a little restaurant serving exquisite food to a maximum of thirty-five diners at six dinners and one luncheon every week. In such a restaurant he would do all the cooking himself and would stand a real chance of being able to offer the finest cuisine in Britain.

Knight feels very strongly that it is the cooking that really matters in a restaurant and that expensive ingredients requiring little or no preparation should be avoided. He despises over-garnishing, especially where the garnish does not really go with the dish it is adorning, and he believes in great variety. At Comrie it was always his boast that a guest could come and have all meals in the hotel for three weeks without any dish being repeated. His menus at Houstoun are always interesting and imaginative as these specialities reveal:

Nettle Kail: Scottish nettle broth
Sea Trout Houstoun: Sea trout baked with
prawns and horseradish and served with a
white wine sauce with added tomato.
Svinai Groudimka Sladkim Sousom: Dressed
loin of pork with a sauce of fruit, honey, and
lemon juice.
Schlosserbuben: Prunes stuffed with almond,
fried in a white-wine batter, rolled in grated
chocolate and served with whipped cream.

There is already one restaurant in Scotland which closely resembles the restaurant of Knight's dreams; it is Inverlochy Castle and it is situated just outside Fort William. There, the dining-room is rarely occupied by more than a dozen people and there is no menu, all meals being by arrangement. Guests have a chat with Grete Hobbs, the Danish-born *patronne,* in the morning, during which she makes some suggestions based on the fresh ingredients that are available that day. Usually, guests are delighted with her ideas but, if they are not, she is always happy to make further recommendations.

Inverlochy Castle which, on one side, looks out over Loch Linnhe and on the other towards the foothills of Ben Nevis, was built in 1863 by Lord Abinger and it remained in his family until 1945 when it was acquired by Joseph Hobbs, the founder of the Great Glen Cattle Ranch. Before he died in 1963, Hobbs expressed a strong wish to his son and daughter-in-law that

55. Inverlochy Castle.

they should make every effort to keep the castle in the family and they readily agreed. However, it is a large home and requires a substantial staff so that by the late 1960s it was becoming clear that if Joseph Hobbs's wish was going to come true, something would have to be done to make the castle help to pay its own way. Now Grete Hobbs was well aware that the castle's greatest asset, apart perhaps from the natural beauty of its surroundings, was Mary Shaw, the cook. Miss Shaw had been born in the outer Orkneys and had spent much of her life acting as a housekeeper in various hotels, and it was while she was working in this capacity at the Imperial Hotel in Fort William that Joseph Hobbs first met her. Then, when his seventy-odd-year-old cook had the misfortune to break her leg in 1960, Hobbs invited Miss Shaw to come to the castle as cook. At first she refused, because she did not know how to cook and had had no training in the culinary arts, but when Hobbs explained that he was a man of simple tastes and would be very happy with an occasional grilled chop or steak, she sportingly agreed to take the job.

After Joseph Hobbs's death, his son and daughter-in-law moved into the castle and a great friendship grew up between Miss Shaw and Mrs. Hobbs. As a child in Denmark, Grete Hobbs had been brought up to enjoy good food and later had travelled widely, sampling restaurants all over Europe. She enjoyed discussing the food at the castle with Mary Shaw and took a great interest in the kitchen, much to the latter's delight. Often Mrs. Hobbs would describe dishes she had particularly enjoyed in restaurants and Mary Shaw would cook them. It soon became clear that she had a most remarkable gift for cooking and, encouraged by Mrs. Hobbs's expert criticism, her

56. Mary Shaw with Mrs. Grete Hobbs in the kitchen at Inverlochy Castle.

standards rose steadily. Guests who came to stay at the castle began to say that they had never eaten so well before anywhere in the world, and this gradually led the Hobbs to think that it might be a good idea to allow guests to come and stay at the castle and pay for the privilege of enjoying the magnificent cuisine. In this way the future of the castle in the Hobbs family would be assured.

Mrs. Hobbs was determined from the start that the castle should not become a hotel in the normal sense of the word and so there are none of the usual trappings of a hotel: there is no reception desk and no bar. Guests staying at the castle congregate in the drawing-room for drinks before lunch and dinner, just as if they were in a house-party.

Being situated in the north of Scotland poses certain supply problems and one of these that particularly bothers Mrs. Hobbs is that she cannot obtain foreign cheeses except in a pre-packed form which, of course, she will not touch. She makes up for this by providing an excellent selection of Scottish cheeses such as Orkney Cheddar, Highland Wild Garlic Cheese, and Caboc.

The problem of obtaining interesting vegetables is overcome by having them grown in the castle grounds. Almost all the vegetables served at the castle are home-grown including aubergines, zucchini, and green peppers. Almost all the fruit is home grown too. The local beef is of such high quality that the castle is able to serve what must be the most succulent *bœuf en croûte* in Britain and the fresh giant prawns from Loch Linnhe are certainly the best that I have ever tasted. Another speciality of the castle, which makes full use of locally obtainable ingredients, is fresh salmon mousse. The only cloud on the horizon is that the Hobbs's have not yet built up a particularly interesting cellar.

There can be no doubt that both Scotsmen and foreign tourists have responded enthusiastically to the efforts of the good restaurants north of the border, and I have no doubt that this will, in time, encourage many more *restaurateurs* to open places where interesting and exciting dishes can be found. It will also encourage groups such as B.T.H. to keep up their standards.

With reasonable luck, it should be possible before too long to begin planning serious gastronomic tours of Scotland and that will be a treat that few gourmets will be able to resist!

Chapter 7

CHINESE FOOD IN BRITAIN

HOW sad it is that, for the majority of British people, Chinese food means little more than *chop suey* and *chow mein* followed by tinned *lychees*. I say how sad because almost everyone who takes the trouble to investigate Chinese food and find out which are the most authentic restaurants and which are the specialities of each region of China, reaches the same conclusion: that real Chinese cuisine is at least the equal of French cooking. We are fortunate in this country in having access to what is almost certainly the best Chinese food in Europe, so we must consider it to be a most important part of our gastronomic scene. It is for this reason that I have decided to devote a separate chapter to the story of the rise and development of Chinese restaurants in Britain.

As we have already seen in the Edwardian chapter, the first Chinese restaurant in Britain (and probably the first in Europe too) was one which is still flourishing today, the Cathay in Piccadilly Circus. The Cathay opened in 1908 and was for some years the only restaurant of its kind in Britain. By the end of the First World War it had been joined by two others, one in Oxford Street and one in Regent Street. Then, a number of restaurants of a more humble variety began to appear during the 1920s chiefly to serve the numerous Chinese sailors who came to this country and badly missed their native cooking. Two important centres of these humbler restaurants were the Limehouse area of London and the dockland area of Liverpool.

By the 1930s, three men had become particularly important in the London Chinese restaurant world; they were Mr. Young, who founded the Hong Kong Restaurant in Shaftesbury Avenue, Mr. Ley-on, who founded a restaurant in Wardour Street which he named after himself, and K. C. Chang who, having worked in an Italian restaurant since 1914, opened an Italian restaurant of his own called Fava which served a variety of Chinese specialities. This restaurant was at No. 13 Frith Street. To give some idea of the impact these men made and of their success, I need only say that when Young died, he left a reported £300,000 which in those days was a fortune, and that Ley-on drove a Rolls-Royce and owned a string of race-horses. When one of them, Kai Ming, won the Derby, the restaurant closed for a few weeks so that the staff, many of whom had placed considerable bets on the animal, could spend some of their winnings on a holiday.

If any single happening was outstandingly significant in the story of the rise of Chinese restaurants in this country, it was the coming of the Second World War. While the war proceeded to devastate Western gastronomy, it gave Chinese restaurants a most remarkable stimulus. London was filled with tens of thousands of American and Commonwealth troops, many of whom had a great liking for Eastern cooking, and these men flocked to the Chinese restaurants. Then, when the Far Eastern seaports were occupied by the Japanese, several thousand Chinese sailors on the high seas were compelled to use Liverpool as their home port. One estimate shows that the Chinese community in that city grew in a matter of weeks in 1941 from 1,000 to almost 6,000. This posed a very difficult problem for the Chinese Embassy in London which was not equipped to deal with the labour problems of so many people. Happily, the embassy had a newcomer on its staff who was equal to dealing with the situation. His name was Kenneth Lo and he belonged to the third generation in his family to work in China's diplomatic service in Britain; his grandfather was one of the first Chinese ever to be knighted. This honour was bestowed upon him by Queen Victoria in recognition of his services as an interpreter to Li Hung Chang who visited Victoria as China's Prime Minister on the occasion of her Diamond Jubilee.

One of Lo's jobs was to help the sailors, many of whom were wounded survivors of the Battle of the Atlantic and therefore had little prospect of returning home before the end of the war, to set up welfare centres, each of which offered extensive catering facilities. Later, a number of sailors to whom Lo had given help and advice at the centres, set up small restaurants of their own. These restaurants catered exclusively for Chinese people and so were largely unknown to the English but they were the first restaurants in this country to offer authentic regional Chinese cooking. The rest of us had to wait until the 1960s before we could enjoy many of the unusual dishes served in these establishments in Liverpool during the war years.

While serving abroad during the war, a great many men in the British forces tasted foreign food for the first time and a large proportion of them found that they liked Eastern cooking. This created a popular demand for Chinese food in Britain after the war for the first time and the Chinese living here were not slow to respond to the demand. Quite a number of restaurants began to open in the late 1940s though it was not until later that the big rush began.

In 1949, Mao Tse Tung's Communist government came to power in China and this caused an exodus of hundreds of thousands of people who migrated to Hong Kong so that the population there almost trebled in a decade. This meant that it was not easy for the refugees to find employment there and so, as Britain did not have very strict immigration laws at that time, many came to England and, finding that there was an ever-increasing demand for Chinese food, began to open restaurants.

Meanwhile K. C. Chang of the Fava Restaurant had moved to Finchley Road and opened the Regency Restaurant. It was only moderately success- ful and Chang found that he missed the atmosphere and bustle of the West End. Nevertheless, he did not move back into central London; instead, he opened one of the early provincial Chinese restaurants, the Oriental Star, in Coventry. This was so successful that he soon opened two more places in Coventry and still found no difficulty in filling all the tables.

In 1951, the British Government officially recognized Mao's régime in China and this left a large proportion of the staff of the Nationalist Chinese Embassy in a most embarrassing position as they had to find a completely new way of earning a living after the years or decades of sheltered life in the diplomatic service. At first, few of them knew what to do, but gradually a number of them drifted into the restaurant business and one of the first places to be born in this way was the Asiatic in Irving Street just off Leicester Square. From this restaurant, which was another that had the help and ad- vice of Kenneth Lo behind it, a chain was born which extended from Hamp- stead to Notting Hill and Swiss Cottage. Later, one of the partners in the

Asiatic left and opened the Rice Bowl in South Kensington which in turn developed a chain of its own. Another partner in the Asiatic also broke away and founded the Good Earth in the King's Road which has since opened sister restaurants in Croydon, Harrow, Ealing, Purley, and elsewhere. Yet another partner opened the Shangri-La in Brompton Road and also the Marco Polo in Chelsea. So the Asiatic must be seen as the fountainhead from which sprouted so many other Chinese restaurants dur- ing the 1950s.

57. Mr. Kenneth Lo.

It was also in the early 1950s that another important group was born when Charlie Cheong opened the Old Friends Restaurant in Limehouse. The group later came to include the New Friends, Good Friends, Young Friends, Local Friends and finally City Friends though the latter is now under separate ownership.

The pattern was not repeated in the provinces where most restaurants were independent and such groups as there were comprised only two or three members. Nevertheless, Chinese food was finding its way into all parts of Britain by the late 1950s and the Manchester area which had had no Chinese restaurants at all just after the war, had several dozen by 1960.

The late fifties and early sixties saw two significant developments in the Chinese restaurant world. First, one or two proprietors began to realize that the *ambiance* and décor of their restaurants was not really worthy of the cooking. One of the first people to open a restaurant with a luxurious décor was Fu Tong who had previously been a 'runner' for the Shell Petroleum Company in Liverpool; that is to say he had had the job of running round the docks and boarding-houses to call the crews together. Fu Tong made the transition from 'runner' to *restaurateur* with great success and his place in Kensington High Street became very fashionable. Soon, his idea was copied by numerous others including Jackie Khoon, the proprietor of the Cathay. He opened a smart restaurant called the Lotus House in Edgware Road and later another of the same name in Brighton. The fashionable China Garden in Brewer Street, Soho, was another of his establishments.

But by far the most important development was the appearance of Pekinese cooking. Until this time, there had only been 'Chinese' restaurants and people had only talked about 'Chinese' food. Today, many people think in terms of *Cantonese* or *Pekinese* restaurants and of *Shanghai* or *Szechuan* dishes, but this is a new phenomenon.

Pekinese cooking began at the Tung Hsing restaurant in Golders Green which was founded in 1961 by two former members of the Chinese Embassy called Dr. Y. S. Chen and Mr. James Liu. As these men employed a well-known chef from the Hopeh Province in Northern China, the province in which Peking is situated, it was only natural that they should offer the cuisine of that region.

Pekinese cooking is recognized as the *haute cuisine* of China and there are many reasons for this. In the first place, the Imperial Palace was situated there and in its heyday it employed between three and four hundred cooks who were capable of laying on the most magnificent banquets ever

58. The Tung Hsing Restaurant
in Golders Green.

seen in China. Secondly, situated just below Inner Mongolia, Peking has benefited from the influence of Chinese Muslims. This is particularly noticeable in roasts and barbecues which form such an important part of Pekinese cuisine although they are not indigenous techniques of cooking. Indeed, the famous Peking Duck is really a Mongolian dish.

Peking Duck is prepared by taking a well-cleaned bird and dipping it momentarily in boiling water. It is then hung up to dry for several hours or overnight. Later a mixture of malt sugar and soya sauce is rubbed all over it and it is roasted so that the skin becomes very crisp on the outside while leaving the flesh underneath moist. Next, it is cut into small pieces, the skin and the flesh being kept separate. When it is brought to the table, each diner takes a pancake and spreads a little plum sauce or sweetened bean paste on to it. He then takes a few pieces of raw spring onion and a little thinly sliced cucumber and lays them in a line across the pancake. Finally, he places several small pieces of duck skin and duck meat on top of the raw vegetables then rolls up the pancake and eats it.

The use of sesame seeds is also very popular in Pekinese cooking and they are used both for savoury and sweet dishes. One example of this is toasted prawns in sesame seeds or, as a pudding, fried apple or banana dipped in melted sugar, sprinkled with sesame seeds and made brittle by a quick immersion in cold water.

Naturally enough, many important Pekinese dishes use other ingredients which are plentiful in the region such as lamb, long celery cabbage, and giant prawns, the latter being found in the mud in the estuary of the Yellow River. From these ingredients come such dishes as quick-fried lamb; small, thin slices of lamb fried and served with leeks and steamed bread. The prawns are dry-fried in their shells and the long cabbage is either cooked in soya sauce and wine or else in chicken broth flavoured with dried shrimps.

It is also from Hopeh Province that two of the most famous and delicate of all Chinese soups come; they are of course, Bird's Nest and Shark's Fin soup. These are both examples of true *haute cuisine* and are only usually served at banquets and special occasions as well they might be considering that the current price of Shark's Fin in England is £10 per pound.

Cantonese cooking which, in an Anglicized form, was the only sort of Chinese food available in England before the Tung Hsing opened, is very different. It does not provide much for roasts or barbecues and it uses a far higher proportion of seafood and far more fruit than Pekinese food. Many people regard *chop suey* as a typical Cantonese dish because it is always found on the menu in these restaurants but in fact it is not a Chinese dish at all – it was created in San Francisco by Chinese cooks who wanted to use up their left-overs to attract Americans and other foreign nationalities into their restaurants. Typical Cantonese fare includes sweet and sour dishes, dumplings containing a mixture of pork with crab or pork with prawns, squid stewed with pork and lychees and sliced steak with oyster sauce.

For a while, the Tung Hsing remained the only Pekinese restaurant in Britain and it had on its staff two remarkable men. The chef, a Mr. Kuo Teh-Lu, was a man of exceptional ability; in 1961 he joined the staff of the restaurant after walking out of the Chinese Embassy in Portland Place as he reportedly could not stand excessive self-criticism sessions. The waiter, a Mr. T. H. Young (no relation of the Young of the Hong Kong Restaurant), came from Shantung Province in Northern China where his father had inherited a share in a restaurant. For a period he had worked there but later moved to a restaurant in Shanghai. Soon after the Communists came to power in China, he went to Hong Kong and worked in its most famous restaurant, the Princes Garden.

In 1963, Young left the Tung Hsing and opened the first of what was to be Britain's most significant group of Chinese restaurants. I say 'most significant' because his restaurants offer both the highest standard of cooking and, between them, every kind of Chinese regional cuisine. This first restaurant was the Richmond Rendezvous – a former steakhouse – and such was the popularity of the Pekinese food it served that within two years, Young and his chef-partner W. S. Chu found it necessary to open an annexe round the corner. Two years later, in 1967, they acquired the Dumpling Inn in Gerrard Street and in the following year, the Gallery

59. Mr. T. H. Young outside the Richmond Rendezvous.

Rendezvous in Beak Street. This restaurant is so named because it is there that Mr. Young displays his fine collection of Chinese paintings. The walls of the restaurant are far too few to accommodate them all at one time so he displays them in rotation. In 1969, the restaurant where he had begun his English career, the Tung Hsing, was added to the group and since then there has followed the Edinburgh Rendezvous, the Soho Rendezvous, the Chelsea Rendezvous, the Chiu Chow Inn, and the Summer Palace at Eastbourne – the latter being probably the largest Chinese restaurant on the south coast.

The Chelsea Rendezvous was called the Yen Hua until Mr. Young acquired it and it was particularly important in being the first restaurant in London to offer Shanghai dishes. It was able to do this for the simple reason that the chef came from that part of China. It is a strange thing but very few people from Shanghai are to be found in the West, fewer than from other regions, and most of those who have come to live in the West are shipping magnates and not chefs. Unfortunately, the Yen Hua did not become very popular and so when Mr. Young took over he had to change the name and also substitute Pekinese and Szechuan dishes for some of the Shanghai specialities. A few Shanghai dishes remain on the menu but for the most part, the great specialities of that region can only be obtained by ordering in advance.

It is a great pity that Shanghai food is so hard to come by in this country as it is delicious. Casseroles are the great speciality of which characteristic examples are: duck casserole flavoured with onion and tangerine, fish balls in clear soup, carp in mutton broth, simmered trout with preserved cabbage and braised, deep-fried eel.

Szechuan dishes are also rarely found in this country; they come from Western China, from near where Chairman Mao was born, and they are the hottest of all Chinese dishes, almost all of them containing substantial quantities of chilli. The use of sesame seeds is also popular in this part of China but, unlike Pekinese cooking where the seeds are usually sprinkled on to the food, in Szechuan dishes the seeds are ground into a sort of jam or paste, not unlike peanut butter, and this is often used as a sauce for poultry and other things. Szechuan cooking also involves a technique called double-cooking; for instance, pork might be boiled first and then sliced and braised in a sauce of black beans and chilli. 'Fish-flavoured' dishes are also popular but this does not mean that the food is actually given a fishy flavour; it is simply that the meat or vegetables are prepared with some of the ingredients that are usually used in cooking fish. The French have a comparable idea, they talk of *moules à l'escargot* although there is no trace of snail to be found in that dish. Szechuan 'fish-flavoured' dishes are served with a sauce containing such ingredients as spring onions, leeks, ginger, garlic, black beans, soya sauce, chilli, and wine.

Szechuan cooking outside China made its début a few years ago in New York where it quickly became the rage. At the time of writing it can only be found in three British restaurants: the Chelsea Rendezvous, Ming Yuan in the King's Road, and the Golden Duck, a restaurant of which we shall be hearing more later.

At present, only one restaurant in Britain specializes in Chiu Chow cooking and that is, of course, the Chiu Chow Inn which opened in Lisle Street, Soho, in 1972. This style of cooking comes from the port of Swatow in South China and the emphasis is on fish and seafoods. Sea bass and lemon sole are steamed and served with various kinds of sauce; one favourite contains sour, unripe plums. These plums have much the same effect as lemon juice but their flavour is far more subtle. Steamed crab is dipped in a sauce of shredded ginger and vinegar and quick-fried sliced fish is flavoured with a preserved vegetable called *tung-choi* which tastes almost exactly like garlic.

Another popular Chiu Chow dish is fish-flavoured chicken. In this case the chicken is not just prepared like fish as in Szechuan cooking, it is actually given a fishy savoury flavour by being braised and served with a sauce made of dried sole. Chiu Chow duck is also delicious: it is simmered in a diluted soya-based master sauce and then sliced or chopped before serving. There are also a number of excellent puddings which come from this region, for instance, steamed, sweetened whole chestnuts that taste very much like *marrons glacés* and sweetened *purée* of yams or *purée* of green beans with syrup.

While T. H. Young was busy building his empire of restaurants, others were not idle. Not long after Young left the Tung Hsing the chef also left and set up a restaurant in Willesden which he called Kuo Yuan. When it had been going for a while, a Russian called Shura Shihwarg who had lived for many years in China visited it and was so excited by Kuo's high standard of cooking that he began to go there regularly and brought some of his friends along such as Sean Connery and Twiggy. Soon, the Press became interested and when the word had got round it became a regular occurrence to see long lines of cars bearing 'C.D.' plates making their way towards Willesden every evening. The restaurant became such a success that Kuo felt he ought to expand. He opened two branches, one in Princes Street near Oxford Circus and one in Richmond, quite near the Richmond Rendezvous, but for some reason they did not really catch on. After a while, Kuo sold them off and decided that he would just continue with Willesden which still retains its high standards.

Another important Chinese *restaurateur* who appeared in the 1960s was Michael Chow. He had not previously been involved in catering as he had been a hairdresser. However, he had a great flair for design and publicity and he realized that one formula which could not fail to be an enormous success would be to combine good Pekinese and other Chinese cooking with a really trendy atmosphere. The result of this concept was 'Mr. Chow' in Knightsbridge which some of the purists regard as not authentic but which most people find great fun. He later opened a second restaurant not very far away which he called Mr. Chow's Montpellier and he has recently opened a Japanese restaurant and Chow Ciao-Bomba in Soho.

Finally, in looking at the great *restaurateurs* of the 1960s, we must come back to Shura Shihwarg, the man who set Kuo on the map by taking all his smart friends up to Willesden. Shura's next appearance in the story came when he helped to set up a Pekinese restaurant in Wembley called Fung Tse Yuan which is run by the Wang family who also have interests in restaurants in Montreal. Soon it was clear that this new restaurant was a great success and this prompted Shura to decide to open a place of his own. He therefore took on a partner called Johnny Chu and opened what he likes to describe as 'London's first Chinese *bistro*': the Golden Duck in Hollywood Road.

60. Shura Shihwarg at the Golden Duck.

Shura was born in Manchuria of Russian parents and he was bilingual in Russian and Chinese from an early age. By the age of eight, as a result of attending the English school at the treaty-port of Tien Tsin, he had become trilingual and this later enabled him to go up to Wadham College, Oxford. His upbringing has given him a very deep love of China and he feels so very much at home with his Chinese partners, friends, and employees in England that they go a long way towards making up for his severance from his birthplace. He is unique in Britain as being the only non-Chinese to own a Chinese restaurant.

Shura called the Golden Duck a *bistro* for two reasons: firstly because he is a Russian and it is, after all, a Russian word and secondly because the restaurant has the décor and *ambiance* of a *bistro*.

'The Achilles heel of Chinese catering outside China,' he says, 'is service and floor management. In China, service is still obliging and hospitable and takes a pride in its function whereas in this country, waiters are hostile.

I always feel about a Chinese waiter that he treats his European customers as if they had been personally responsible for the Opium Wars. The average Chinese restaurant has been a place which served tepidly exotic food (cheap as well) in a totally anonymous setting and in an atmosphere of sullen hostility which made one choke on one's crispy noodle.'

And so Shura created a *bistro* because he felt that Chinese waiters were well suited to an informal atmosphere. In colourful shirts and in very dim light his staff serve exquisite Pekinese dishes to a 'trendy' clientele.

The Golden Duck is highly original in its décor. Shura has very strong views on this: 'The décor of a good Chinese restaurant is too important to leave to the Chinese. In China restaurants have a lot of character but not much in the way of design since in a country afflicted with recurrent famine and distinguished by the excellence of its cuisines, there seems to be no point in providing atmospheric effects. But in England, there is no reason why a restaurant shouldn't emanate a little personality and atmosphere.'

Shura has used a bright colour scheme based on the traditional *motives* of the Temple of Heaven with a strong underlying feeling of European pop art.

There is just one more aspect of Chinese food in Britain that must be looked at and that is snack food. There are now a number of Chinese noodle shops in Soho which offer very cheap, tasty one-course meals consisting of roast meat and vegetables on noodles or rice. But for those who like even their snacks to be exciting, I would recommend restaurants offering a range of *Dim Sum*. *Dim Sum* is the general name given to the various types of steamed dumpling and croquettes which the Chinese regard as suitable for high tea or just as a light meal. As most items of *Dim Sum* cost no more than 25p per portion, two people can have a lunch comprising six varieties of dumplings for about 75p per person. Typical items are meat dumplings, pork dumplings, prawns on toast, spare ribs with black beans, steamed buns filled with roast pork or chicken and gravy and wan tun which are rather like thin-skinned ravioli. A number of Cantonese restaurants, particularly in Soho, offer a range of *Dim Sum* and to try them is a pleasant experience although they are not as substantial or as sophisticated as most of the other dishes we have looked at.

It is certainly impressive to see how in a little over twenty years, Chinese food has come to form such an important part of our gastronomic scene. Far more people in this country have eaten in Chinese restaurants than in, say, Greek or Italian ones and they do offer the highest level of gastronomy at the lowest price. Egon Ronay goes so far as to say that he wonders if people really appreciate just how good the standard of cooking is in the Chinese restaurants they visit. He also says that the general standard of Chinese restaurants is higher than the general standard of French restaurants in this country.

I should feel very happy if some of those who have looked through this chapter have been sufficiently intrigued by what they have read to want to take a closer look at Chinese food and it therefore seems a good idea to offer a little practical advice about how to do so. Kenneth Lo has written more books on Chinese food than anyone else and his paperback published by Penguin Books called *Chinese Food* will, for a few pence, provide its readers with a very good general understanding of the subject and will also help them to know how to get the most out of the restaurants they visit.

GENERAL ADVICE:

1. Try to go in parties of, say, four or more. Of course it is perfectly possible for two to have a very enjoyable meal but with larger parties, the variety of dishes can obviously be far greater. Each person should have his own soup and rice but share everything else.

2. Try to order a well-balanced range of dishes – make sure that your order includes some fish, meat, poultry, and vegetable. Also make sure that the dishes are different in character; it is a mistake to order too high a proportion of sweet and sour or hot peppery dishes but, equally, you do not want to confine yourself to plain bland ones.

3. Generally speaking, it is rather a waste to drink good wine with Chinese food. If you particularly enjoy drinking wine, then stick to *saké* which although expensive is the ideal complement to Chinese food.

Chinese Regional Cooking in London:

Here is a list drawn up in consultation with Mr. Lo of London restaurants serving authentic regional Chinese food. Of course, these are not the only good ones but the list will act as a preliminary guide. For details of telephone numbers, prices, etc., I suggest you consult either Egon Ronay's *Guide* or the *Good Food Guide*.

Pekinese:

Kuo Yuan (Willesden)
Lee Yuan (Earls Court Road)
Chelsea Rendezvous (Sydney Street, S.W.3)
Gallery Rendezvous (Beak Street, W.1)

Golden Duck (Hollywood Road, S.W.10)
Soho Rendezvous (Romilly Street, W.1)
Dumpling Inn (Gerrard Street, W.1)
Tung Hsing (Golders Green)

Cantonese:

Lee Ho Fook (Gerrard Street, W.1)
Lee Ho Fook (Wardour Street, W.1)
Chen Chang Ku (Wardour Street, W.1)
City Friends (Creed Lane, E.C.4)
Kam Tong (Queensway, W.2)

Lido Restaurant (Gerrard Street, W.1)
Marco Polo (Kings Road, S.W.3)
Loon Fung (Gerrard Street, W.1)
Chuen Chang Ku (Lisle Street, W.1)
Chuen Chang Ku (Wardour Street, W.1)

Szechuan: (Only a few Szechuan dishes will normally be readily available, for others you will have to order in advance)

Chelsea Rendezvous (Sydney Street, S.W.3)
Golden Duck (Hollywood Road, S.W.10)
Ming Yuan (Kings Road, S.W.3)

Shanghai:

Chelsea Rendezvous (Sydney Street, S.W.3)
(Only a few Shanghai dishes are on the menu, for the rest you have to order in advance.)

Chiu Chow (or Swatow):

Chiu Chow Inn (Lisle Street, W.1)

Dim Sum:

Chen Chang Ku (Wardour Street, W.1)
Lido Restaurant (Gerrard Street, W.1)

Loon Fung (Gerrard Street, W.1)
Lee Ho Fook (Gerrard Street, W.1)
Kam Tong (Queensway, W.2)

Chinese Food Outside London:

The standard of cooking in the provinces is slightly lower though there are certainly exceptions. Most provincial restaurants still call themselves simply 'Chinese' and do not offer anything outside what one might call the Anglo-Cantonese repertoire of dishes but there are now good Pekinese restaurants in Richmond, Wembley, Liverpool, Ely, Edinburgh, Birmingham, Mitcham, and a few other places. The reason for the rather limited repertoire of many provincial restaurants is that with no large concentration of Chinese population outside London there is no great call for more interesting and authentic dishes. However, if you are planning a Chinese dinner for four or more people, I would strongly advise you to go and consult the manager of your local restaurant a few days in advance. The chances are that if you tell him how much you are prepared to spend per person (and it should be between £1·75 and £3) and ask him to arrange the menu for you, he will come up with a surprisingly good feast. In most cases the chefs have the necessary skill to produce a really good meal but customers do not know how to order a well-balanced dinner or think they know and proceed to order badly.

Chapter 8

CONCLUSION

THE present high standard of restaurants in Britain is a great achievement. Since the last war good food has penetrated to the most remote corners of the country, and in London virtually every nationality of food is offered and often these examples of national cuisine are of a very high quality. Gourmets who travel regularly to Greece have told me that they consider the White Tower in Soho to be the greatest Greek restaurant in the world, while my own travels in Hungary have led me to realize that there is nothing in that country to equal the Gay Hussar (which is also is Soho). French cooking in the English provinces has reached a very high level: I should like to find a restaurant in France whose *quenelles de saumon à la crême* could surpass those offered at Thornbury Castle or whose *coq au vin* could outshine that offered at the Box Tree Cottage.

Another cause for celebration is that a considerably higher proportion of the population than ever before can now afford to eat in restaurants and, thanks to this greater prosperity and the increase in foreign travel, more and more people now know something about food and wine and take a real interest in it. Our etiquette has changed, so that it has become socially acceptable to talk about food and to praise our hostesses whenever we are given something of particular merit. With the publication of the *Michelin Guide* in England, we now have three restaurant guides of particular merit, and these help to keep *restaurateurs* on their toes. Yes, it has been a very satisfactory period in the history of British gastronomy but I fear that the future is by no means a rosy one.

The crisis is already at hand. Egon Ronay told me recently that in his opinion standards reached a peak in 1970 or 1971 since when there has been no improvement. So far they have not begun to decline but it is a sinister sign that they are standing still. Quentin Crewe, writing in the July 1973 issue of his *Private File* commented: 'It seems to me that we have reached a watershed beyond which things can never get better and will almost certainly get worse.'

The cause of all this gloom and pessimism is that *restaurateurs* at the moment face some very serious problems, of which the worst is the shortage of staff. We have never been good at producing our own waiters and for many years we have relied to a great extent on employing foreign staff. In recent years, however, many of the foreign countries from which our staff used to come, such as France and Italy, have had restaurant booms of their own and consequently the number of people from these countries seeking jobs in Britain has fallen sharply. It probably would still be possible to attract people from Greece and Portugal but the E.E.C. rules make this almost impossible.

The staff shortage produces one particularly serious consequence: a lack of discipline. Many proprietors are too frightened of losing staff to demand high standards from them. This is especially noticeable in New York where waiters in the best restaurants are surly and chefs are sloppy. This situation is beginning to appear in this country and may soon begin to spoil the atmosphere of our restaurants.

Of course the worst aspect of the staff shortage is the acute shortage of chefs, especially of skilful ones. The chef's life is a hard one; the hours are long, years of training are required and working conditions are often uncomfortable. Not unnaturally, fewer and fewer people are coming forward for this kind of work and even among the few that do come forward, only a very small percentage bother to obtain a thorough training as they know that they can easily find a job as soon as they have learned to grill a steak or make an apple pie. A number of important changes will have to be made now if we are going to have any good chefs at all in this country in a few years' time.

First, chefs' pay will have to come into line with the rates offered in other countries. At present we do not pay rates comparable to those offered by many of our fellow members in the Common Market. Secondly, we must make an effort to improve chefs' working conditions and one way in which this can be done is to reduce the number of working hours. This has already been done at a number of restaurants such as the Capital Hotel in Basil Street, Le Gavroche, and Carrier's where kitchen staff are never called upon to prepare more than one meal a day. Conditions could also be improved by the use of better equipment, ventilation, and lighting in many of our more old-fashioned kitchens.

Another aspect of the chef's job which should be improved is his status. This, obviously, is far harder to improve than anything else but in France, if a *bourgeois* dinner party is given, a good chef may well be invited to join the local mayor, bank manager, and solicitor as a guest at the dinner table. In France he is regarded as a true artist, almost as if he were a musician or a sculptor. In England we tend to think of chefs as being rather ill-shaven, inferior beings and very rarely treat them with the same respect as we would accord to a bank manager, let alone an artist.

Nick Clarke has suggested that the whole tone of the profession could be raised by setting up a really prestigious academy of gastronomy but so far no such academy has been created.

The standard of wine waiters in British restaurants has always been low and there are signs that it might fall lower still. More than thirty years ago when Marcel Boulestin wrote his book *Ease and Endurance** he complained: 'There are few wine waiters in England, wine being usually served by one of the *maîtres d'hôtel* with only a smattering of knowledge.' He also mentions a story of a waiter in a provincial hotel who served him an abominably corked bottle of Lafite and then confided to him, 'What do you expect, sir, when the cellarman keeps the bottles lying down so that the wine touches the corks?' Things are just as bad as that today and more often than not the vitally important job of *sommelier* is given to a young man who, far from being able to tell you whether a Pommerol or a St. Julian would go better with your Duck, does not even know whether these wines come from France or Spain. There are, of course, some exceptions to this: a Guild of *Sommeliers* was started from the Connaught Hotel a few years ago with the enthusiastic encouragement of Rudolph Richard. The Guild meets regularly to taste and talk about wines, to discuss wine books and to exchange views on various vintages. The Connaught also sends its *sommeliers* to the vineyards of France and Germany from time to time to keep them up to date with the latest developments in the wine world had to stimulate their enthusiasm. Joseph Berkmann of the Genevieve Group of restaurants is another proprietor who sends his wine waiters to France but then this is only natural for he is, among other things, wine correspondent of the *Daily Mail* and therefore appreciates the importance of these things. If restaurants are going to maintain their standards it is essential that the managements of some of the more money-conscious, greedy ones should realize the importance of inspiring their *sommeliers* and sacrifice, if necessary, a little profit to do this!

Enthusiasm is catching and I believe that if a *patron* or a manager can make his kitchen and cellar staff enthusiastic, the chances are that much of this will rub off on the waiters. If a waiter spends his whole time dishing out inferior food to customers who do not care what they eat, who can blame him for being surly and off-hand? But if the dishes are good and the custo-

* Marcel Boulestin, *Ease and Endurance* translated by Robin Adair (Home and van Thal, 1948).

mers are excited by what is set before them the waiter will often share their pleasure with them.

The second fundamental problem facing restaurants today is the supply situation. There is only so much fillet steak, so much sole and so many lobsters to go round and now that more and more people want them, the prices are soaring. The supply situation is almost more depressing in the wine world where the price of good claret and champagne has more than doubled in the last two or three years. This in turn has meant that the slightly less good wines, such as Côtes du Rhone, have been in far greater demand than ever before and consequently they too are increasing in cost. Egon Ronay predicts that the effect of these price increases, together with the substantial wage increases which are going to have to come along shortly, will result in the cost of a first-class dinner in London rising in the next year or so to well over £20. I am already being presented with bills in the upper thirties for dinners for two in London. When the £20 dinner becomes the order of the day, many restaurants will only cater for business entertaining and the atmosphere will change for the worse. The only hope of salvation here is that we might, as a nation, decide to fall into line with French habits and spend a larger proportion of our income on eating out. As Derek Cooper said in his *Bad Food Guide**: 'We spend money not on eating well, but on decorating our homes, on crazy paving, and three-piece suites.' If this were to change there would be more hope for the future of good restaurants in this country.

The wine price explosion is one that particularly saddens me because it seems that the best wine in the world is being drunk by people who, for the most part, are buying it for the wrong reasons. The Japanese are so rich nowadays that they have to spend their money on something and many of them think that *premier cru* clarets provide a useful outlet for their millions of surplus yen. None of the Japanese people I have spoken to have even the slightest knowledge of wine. They store it badly and they drink it with unsuitable foods at unsuitable temperatures. All they know is that if the name Rothschild appears somewhere on the label, it must be all right. They are quite open about this and, though they are a people whom I respect very much, I wish that they would stick to *saké* and that the rich American ladies who offer two-year-old first growths to their women's clubs would buy their home-grown Californian wines instead.

Health is a big consideration in many people's lives these days and I sometimes wonder what effect this might have on our restaurants. As the

* *The Bad Food Guide* (Routledge, 1967).

greatest gourmet of the century, André Simon, lived to the ripe old age of ninety-three, I really cannot see why people should worry and my advice, for what it is worth, is to get on with life and enjoy yourself. But are we all going to become so conscious of cholesterol and calory counts that we shall exist on synthetic foods in the future? Philippa Pullar had this to say in her book *Consuming Passions**: 'As the years passed into the sixties an awkward fact was observed. There was malnutrition in the country, malnutrition and disease. But these were due to no shortage or failure of harvest. Obversely this was malnutrition owed to surfeit. A new disease had entered the affluent society: obesity.' Well, I quite agree that it is not pleasant to be fat but it is perfectly possible to eat well without growing fat. It is largely a matter of balancing a number of plain light meals with a few delicious rich ones. It is surely ridiculous to go through life always avoiding sauces with cream or butter when these can be fully compensated for by taking a little exercise and by cutting out foods that are not worth getting fat for!

Nevertheless, Miss Pullar is undoubtedly right when she goes on to say, 'Humans are perverse creatures, food is plentiful so it is no longer a sign of prestige to be plump.' As a result, men and women of all ages are now trying to live off plain grills and roasts, to cut out puddings and to avoid all the minor delicious trimmings that make a good dinner particularly enjoyable. Happily, one has seen that despite all the warnings that cigarette smoking may be harmful to one's health, the habit of smoking is as popular as ever, so I very much doubt that considerations of health will in the long run drive all fattening dishes off our menus. Besides, the fact that a particular dish may be fattening is not its only potential health hazard. What could be more slimming than a plain grilled steak? Yet we are told that the cholesterol content of a good steak is alarmingly high. Again, dieters often go for cold chicken salad, but in this age, when so many chickens come from broiler houses, is not the health risk of eating these birds higher than the risk of getting fat? There is some evidence that hormones used to fatten broiler animals may lodge in the meat with harmful effects on those who eat it. There is also evidence that intensively-reared animals build up large quantities of protein-containing saturated fat. This kind of protein is not body-building like normal protein; it only provides energy.† I was very pleased when I read about the health hazards of broiler meat because it will mean in the long run that greater efforts will be made to expand free-range production.

* *Consuming Passions* (Hamish Hamilton, 1971).
† See HORIZON, 24 January 1970.

Another interesting technical development has been the creation of artificial steak and chicken out of woven soya-bean fibres with added fat and flavour. This 'meat' will no doubt have a very low cholesterol content but woe betide the first restaurant that serves it up to me.

Enough said about the hazards facing *restaurateurs*: let us now turn to the even more important matter of the shape of restaurants to come. All the indications at present are that London restaurants in general, large restaurants and restaurants owned by groups are the most likely to decline over the next few years. The real hope for good food in the future lies with restaurants run by *chef-patrons*, but before we look at this type of establishment, I would like to discuss the second grade of restaurants in the future which will be highly mechanized and supplied from central kitchens. If there are still going to be restaurants where reasonably good food can be found at an acceptable price, they will have to work on this principle, for it is a principle that to a great extent eliminates wastage of food, labour, and equipment. This, I am sure, will alarm many readers but before they worry too much, I must point out that some hope does lie in the latest technical developments which are making it possible to narrow the gap in quality between freshly prepared dishes and expertly-frozen reheated ones. Of course, the distinction will never disappear; we will always have to go to a restaurant run by a *chef-patron* to eat really well, but the average standards of the more ordinary establishments could actually be raised by these technical innovations. The advantages of centralized preparation of food are obvious. On a slack night a restaurant is most unlikely to occupy fully the services of its sauce, vegetable, pastry, and grill chefs, while on a really busy night they may be overstretched and the quality of the meal might consequently suffer. When food is prepared in a central kitchen, portion control is very easy to arrange and so costings can be exact; nothing is prepared in a rush and equally no labour is wasted as there are neither slack times nor sudden rushes. The trouble has been that food prepared in this way, then frozen and distributed, has been tasteless and has often had an unsatisfactory texture. It is possible that technology is now close to solving these problems. I for one used to be a violent opponent of frozen foods, but since I have met Paul Leyton of the Miners' Arms at Priddy in Somerset and eaten at his restaurant, I have had to change my mind. Mr. Leyton found, when he took over the Miners' Arms in 1961, that its position in a remote corner of Somerset caused all sorts of serious difficulties. As the number of persons eating at the restaurant varied greatly from day to day, it was very difficult to know what was the right number of staff to employ. It was also very difficult to know what quantities of food to prepare as, although he has always tried to cook each dish to order, there are many dishes that require such lengthy preparation that unless some of it is done before the customer arrives, it is simply not possible to serve him without keeping him waiting for more than an hour. Another very serious problem was that he could not easily obtain fresh supplies daily. His alternatives were thus either to restrict the choice enormously or to offer slightly tired ingredients. He certainly never chose the latter alternative, but immediately began to look for ways round the problem. As a former scientist he was in a good position to apply his mind to the difficulty and he realized that if he could find improved ways of freezing and reheating his worries would be over.

Leyton's first reason for supposing that freezing could produce extremely satisfactory results if expertly used came about almost by accident. In 1962 a farm just near him suddenly found that a most enormous mushroom crop had grown in one of its fields. As a result, the farmer's wife begged the restaurant to take as much of the crop as possible and the only storage room available was in one of the large deep freezes. Some time later, Leyton took out some of the frozen mushrooms and put them in a dish in the oven. Ten minutes later he opened the oven door and 'the whole kitchen was suffused with an overpowering aroma of mushrooms . . . Field mushrooms, which these were, are pretty flavoursome anyway but the flavour of these that I had thawed was overpowering. So started a slow tick-ticking process in my head. If freezing could so enhance the flavour of field mushrooms, could it do something for the otherwise unnoticeable flavour of the cultivated variety?' Soon Leyton had proved that freezing could, in certain circumstances enrich the flavour of some foods and he went on from there to apply his techniques to all sorts of things. Now all his soups and sauces are frozen and, as one who has tasted many of them, I would never have guessed it.

Nicholas Clarke of 'Nick's Diner' fame is another who wants to apply his knowledge of gastronomy to freezing. It is his current ambition to set up a number of eating-houses where a variety of truly gastronomic dishes, prepared and frozen in a central kitchen, could be expertly reheated, garnished, and served. This, in effect, would mean that an enthusiastic couple could run a small restaurant entirely on their own and serve very acceptable and imaginative food at modest prices. Nick's idea is that his central kitchen should have a repertoire of about 100 dishes of which a dozen or so would be available at any one time. Under this system it would be very easy to bring one or two warming dishes on to the menu if the weather suddenly turned cold or to introduce some simple light ones if it suddenly became hot.

A number of the frozen dishes, probably most in fact, would be reheated in microwave ovens. When I was told that, I made a mental note that I would never eat in any of these restaurants because I usually find that microwaves leave the food hot inside but pallid and rather soggy on the outside. My fears have, however, been largely proved groundless since a new kind of microwave oven has been introduced which heats the inside of whatever is placed inside it in the usual way but which also has radiant and convector heat to brown the crust and remove any excess moisture on the outside.

For those who will not eat frozen food on principle and for those who can afford to pay rather more for their meals the answer will lie in finding good restaurants having a *chef-patron*. In this age where more and more jobs are becoming purely mechanical, an increasing number of people are anxious to 'do their own thing' and one outlet for people with such aspirations is to become a *restaurateur*. It is in this sort of establishment that I believe the real future of gastronomy in Britain lies. Often, because of high rates, rents, and other basic costs, such places will be situated in the country but this will not matter provided that there are enough of them to cover the whole country. The *chef-patron* will probably always try to obtain fresh ingredients. Whenever possible he will go to local farmers and market gardeners to obtain his raw materials and, because he loves his work and is not just doing it for a living, the chances are that he will very rarely, if ever, cut corners. Of course, this kind of proprietor does exist in the cities too, but in the whole of London I have so far only discovered one restaurant where the proprietors regularly go out to market to buy food every day: Le Français in Fulham Road.

In order to be profitable, these *chef-patron* restaurants will have to offer a very limited menu with little or no choice. I believe that there will be a great increase in the number of places offering fixed-price menus as in France and in many cases this might be a change for the better. This system already exists at such places as Houstoun House near Edinburgh and at Miller Howe at Windermere. Many of these places will also probably have to follow the example of Paul Leyton and offer good-value house wines with perhaps a few exciting bottles for rich connoisseurs. Unless this happens, it will soon become impossible for any except the very rich to drink good wine regularly. I believe that a proprietor is doing his guests a great service in choosing a really good house-wine and it is one of the few ways in which he can help to keep bills lower. It also enables him to tie up far less capital in having an enormous cellar, while the few customers who are prepared to pay vast prices to drink really well will still be satisfied as long as he keeps just a few cases of special bottles.

It is regrettable that just at the moment when we, as a nation, are for the first time becoming keen on our food and eager to learn about wine, we should be confronted with a serious risk of falling standards and rising prices. The two types of restaurant that I have suggested in this chapter are by no means ideal but they are a sensible compromise. They will ensure that we continue to eat good food and drink acceptable wines without having to pay exorbitant prices for them. Of course I shall be very sad to see the passing of many of our old-established restaurants but I am glad at least to think that gastronomy in Britain need never die.

APPENDIX

SNAIL'S TALE

A humble life of peace I lead,
I injure none in word nor deed
And gladly let the mad world go by;

I love my fellows, every one,
I crave no place in the sun,
A meek and lowly creature am I.

To some I am a thing of scorn
And many can't abide me
And now I find my little house
No longer serves to hide me

For gastronomic tastes agree
That fat and juicy snails like me
Make corpusses devine delicti.

In times that have, alas, gone by
Our only threat came from the sky, –
A predatory blackbird or thrush,

And in high Mendip's thinner air
Such helicidal birds are rare
And life for us was rosy and lush.

But now those seem such happy times
With other snails to play with
For gastropodoniverous crimes
Have left me none to stay with;

No horns erect, no sticky tracts,
No chums to share life's thrilling facts;
No longer fit and able,
They grace some gourmet's table
Drowned in oleaginous mush.

PAUL LEYTON, *patron* of
The Miners' Arms, Priddy

THE LIQUOR OF BRAY

(Written for the Tenth Anniversary of the Opening of the
Hind's Head)

When George the Fifth was still our King
   A knowing friend of mine said:
'You cannot do a better thing
   Than join me at the Hind's Head.
Let Tio Pepe start the feast
   And Hine's Old Cognac crown it;
The food between will take at least
   A dozen flasks to drown it.
For this is truth, that I'll maintain
Until my dying day, Sir:
That ne'er was wine, in any reign,
   As good as the Liquor of Bray, Sir.'

Some people have Teutonic tastes;
   It well may be that those'll
Prefer to line their portly waists
   With perfumed Hock or Mosel.
Let Rauenthaler crown their glass,
   Or, if they prefer the option,
They can from their drop of Sherry pass
   To Piesporter Goldtröpfchen.*
For this is truth, that I'll maintain
   Until my dying day, Sir:
That ne'er was wine, in any reign,
   As good as the Liquor of Bray, Sir.

If Burgundy be your delight
   Explain to me what dastard
Contrived to sin against the light
   And call this Montrachet 'Bastard.'
Or if it be red wine we pour
   I set the choice between ye
Of noble Richebourg Nineteen-Four
   Or Nineteen-Seven Musigny.
For this is truth, that I'll maintain
   Until my dying day, Sir:
That ne'er was wine, in any reign,
   As good as the Liquor of Bray, Sir.

* I know, I know! this is meant to be a humorous poem.

But if your meal be one of state,
  Or special jubilation,
With Krug '28 beside your plate
  You'll rise to the occasion.
If Mumm's the word, let it be heard,
  Lest thirst should make the bride sick;
On honeymoon you call the tune
  If you pay the Piper-Heidsieck.
For this is truth, that I'll maintain
  Until my dying day, Sir:
That ne'er was wine in any reign,
  As good as the Liquor of Bray, Sir.

Within so English a resort
  You'll find that the most sober
Will take his share of a bottle of Port
  Till April, since October.
And here be Ports to tempt from the sea
  The most persistent sailor.
The Cockburn and Croft will do for me,
  And you'll have the excellent Taylor.
For this is truth, that I'll maintain,
  Until my dying day, Sir:
That ne'er was wine, in any reign,
  As good as the Liquor of Bray, Sir.

But wise men know the glass to choose,
  And I my fealty owe, Sir,
(Though other wines I shan't refuse!)
  To the Red Wine of Bordeaux, Sir.
And so I deem it only meet
  To dedicate my poem
To the 1864 Lafite,
  Drunk from a Jeroboam.
For this is truth, that I'll maintain
  Until my dying day, Sir:
That ne'er was wine, in any reign,
  As good as the Liquor of Bray, Sir.

The souls of the just shall rise to Heaven;
   And, 'mid the angel chorus,
I hope that to us it may be given
   To find our good wine before us.
While, if we sometimes damned to Hell
   Our corked or doubtful bottles,
They *might* reach a few of us there as well;
   Right glad to wet our throttles!
So this is truth, that I'll maintain
   Until my dying day, Sir:
That ne'er was wine, in any reign,
   As good as the Liquor of Bray, Sir.

INDEX